EXTRAORDINARY RECIPES FROM

ATLANTA CHEF'S TABLE

THE BIG PEACH

KATE PARHAM KORDSMEIER
Photography by Heidi Geldhauser

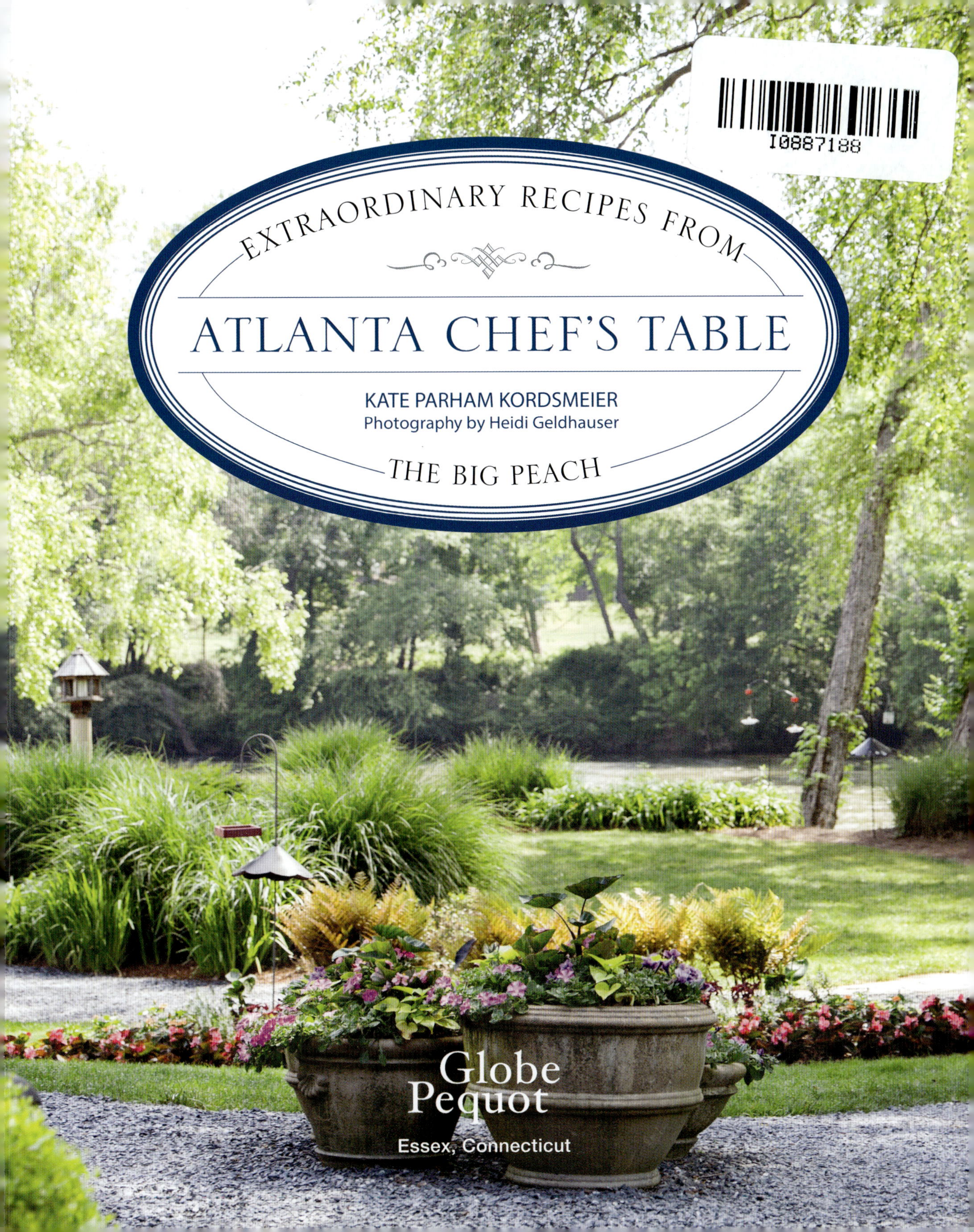

Globe Pequot
Essex, Connecticut

Globe Pequot

An imprint of
The Globe Pequot Publishing Group, Inc.
64 South Main Street
Essex, CT 06426
www.globepequot.com

Distributed by NATIONAL BOOK NETWORK

Paperback edition 2025

All photography by Heidi Geldhauser

British Library Cataloguing in Publication Information available

Library of Congress Cataloging-in-Publication Data

Kordsmeier, Kate Parham.
Atlanta chef's table : extraordinary recipes from the Big Peach / Kate Parham Kordsmeier ; photography by Heidi Geldhauser.
pages cm
Includes index.
1. Cooking—Georgia—Atlanta. 2. Restaurants—Georgia—Atlanta—Guidebooks. I. Title.
TX715.K7464 2015
641.59758'231—dc23
2014040149

ISBN 9781493006335 (hardback)
ISBN 9781493092215 (paperback)
ISBN 9781493016099 (ebook)

∞™ The paper used in this publication meets the minimum requirements of American National Standard for Information Sciences—Permanence of Paper for Printed Library Materials, ANSI/NISO Z39.48-1992.

Restaurants and chefs often come and go, and menus are ever changing. We recommend you call ahead to obtain current information before visiting any of the establishments in this book.

For my mom, who instilled in me a love of food and showed me that cooking is caring. And to Julia Child—you were right: People who love to eat are always the best people.

Contents

Recipes by Course

Breakfast

Soups & Salads

Appetizers & Sides

Burgers, Sandwiches & Pizza

Main Dishes

Desserts

Drinks

Acknowledgments

Writing this book couldn't have come at a better time. After relocating back to my hometown of Atlanta after many years away, it was exactly what I needed to become reacquainted with the vibrant dining scene and inspiring chefs and restaurateurs in the city. This book is truly for them—I couldn't have written it without their unwavering passion for putting good food on the table and their generosity of spirit in sharing their recipes with us. Likewise, I'd like to thank the restaurant publicists who helped me collect all the recipes, schedule dozens of photo shoots, line up interviews and tours, and mostly answer what I'm sure felt like a thousand e-mails from me.

To Heidi: This book wouldn't work without your incredible photos. You have filled these pages with such beauty and wonder, and I am forever grateful for your partnership in this project.

I'd also like to thank my editor, Tracee, who always knew what she wanted and helped me execute that vision in the kindest way possible. Tracee, our industry needs more editors like you!

And finally to my husband, my friends, and my family, who listened to me chatter incessantly about Atlanta restaurants. I know I was in constant fear of missing my deadlines, and your support is truly what allowed me to actually meet them. They say it takes a village—I believe nothing to be more true. Thank you all for bringing this book into existence and making it so wonderful.

Introduction

I was born in Buckhead, my first, formative years spent on a charming street just off Roswell Road. I can remember watching my parents get dressed up to go eat at Pano's & Paul's and Nikolai's Roof. They seemed to be the only good restaurants in Atlanta at the time. Forget about eating out well when we moved to suburbia in 1995—the Cheesecake Factory was as good as it got in Alpharetta.

Eventually, I moved away for college to quirky Athens, spent a summer studying in Verona, Italy, and another interning at a magazine in Los Angeles before heading to Dallas and then back east to Washington, DC. Each of these cities had a food scene I knew to be far superior to what I had left back in Atlanta. Or rather, what I thought I left. The last time I ate in Atlanta was in a different millennium, so when I moved back to the Big Peach in 2013, I was shocked. The city was an entirely different place than the one I'd left just seven years prior.

I should've known. I'd been reading about chefs like Anne Quatrano and Linton Hopkins, two pioneers who transformed Atlanta's fine-dining landscape with their farm-to-table restaurants (Bacchanalia and Restaurant Eugene, respectively) light-years before the philosophy was a trendy, overused buzzword. Back when it actually meant something.

But it wasn't just the *local and seasonal* mind-set that had taken hold of Atlanta. It was the sheer number of restaurants in the city, the majority of which were now owned by chefs rather than corporate entities. Chefs like Kevin Rathbun, Hugh Acheson, Ford Fry, Richard Blais, and Kevin Gillespie, who put Atlanta on the map with their TV appearances, award-winning cookbooks, slew of James Beard nods, and, of course, their delicious food. Chefs like Bruce Logue, Robert Phalen, Todd Ginsberg, Billy Allin, and Steven Satterfield who opened small neighborhood spots that carried a big made-from-scratch stick. Chefs like Asha Gomez, Meherwan Irani, Fuyuhiko Ito, Eddie Hernandez, and Luca Varuni who brought the food from their far-off homelands to the streets of Atlanta.

Streets in formerly forsaken neighborhoods few had been brave enough to enter previously. "People want to get out of those glitzy areas and into something that's real," says Ford Fry, owner of five of Atlanta's most popular restaurants. He's right. Today, you'll find some of the city's best restaurants in the most unexpected of locales—from strip malls to riverfronts, shady street corners to ritzy condos. Many set up shop in converted gas stations, cotton mills, and railroad cars. No longer does Buckhead have a stronghold on the city's dining scene. Today, Atlantans are eating in Inman Park, Old Fourth Ward, Decatur, the Westside, Virginia Highlands, Grant Park, and Buford Highway, all neighborhoods with a story to tell. Neighborhoods are now the destination, the host, rather than a single restaurant. Start at one spot for cocktails, move onto its neighbor for dinner, and then next door for a night cap. No reservations required—if one spot can't take you, there's always someone else nearby who can.

Yes, Atlanta has come a long way; yet even still, when I tell people I live in Atlanta, I'm often asked what we eat "down here." People are shocked to hear our plates aren't just sticks of butter (thanks a lot, Paula Deen). What they don't realize is how diverse this melting pot of a city truly is. "Atlanta is a city of transplants, with tons of influences from other cities and adventurous diners," says Eli Kirshtein, chef-owner of The Luminary. So what's for dinner in the Big Peach?

I think Gunshow owner Kevin Gillespie said it best: "The local food movement has taken hold, people are excited again about true Southern cooking, and chefs are building their own places where they put themselves onto the plate. Look at Bruce Logue—what he does at BoccaLupo is just phenomenal. He lifts pasta to a whole new stratosphere. Linton Hopkins understands how to keep old and traditional and mix in new and modern with grace and beauty. Anne Quatrano, who's always had the best taste in town, may not be new, but she's always current. And then there's the hole-in-the wall Buford Highway spots. That's the South we live in these days. Vietnamese food cooked there is just as Southern as shrimp and grits. Our cuisine has always been made up of learning from these other people—they start out as visitors and become your family."

I couldn't be more thrilled to be a part of Atlanta's family. It's an exciting time to be a Southerner, perhaps nowhere more so than in Atlanta, the nucleus of the New South. Gone are the days of stale, overdone dishes. In their place: new techniques, new

ingredients, new chefs. Take it from Robert Phalen, chef-owner of One Eared Stag: "A lot of us grew up cooking in kitchens where the thing was to buy the best possible product. Now we step back and we make the best product. Instead of sourcing out delicious cheese that costs $32 an ounce, we make our own cheese. We harvest the roe sacks from the fish we get in, we make our own sausage. We're not just purveyors; we're going back to the roots of how food used to be and figuring out how to do stuff, rather than just buy stuff." Amen.

And cocktails. Oh the cocktails. I've been blown away by the innovation in Atlanta's cocktail scene—I'm enamored by the bar program at Kimball House in Decatur, where dangerously delicious concoctions go down best in between slurps of fresh oysters. Kimball House is also one of the few (maybe the only) bars in town offering classic absinthe service (they've got a dozen spirits to choose from). Just down the street, Paul Calvert's Paper Plane is another watering hole frequented by my friends and me. Their ever-changing cocktail list never fails to thrill, nor does Jerry Slater's potent libations at H. Harper Station. There's stellar beer in Atlanta, too. From brewpubs like Wrecking Bar and Brick Store Pub to breweries like Red Brick and SweetWater, there's no shortage of sips in this town.

My goal with this book is to introduce you to some of these revolutionary restaurants, share their incredible stories with you, and give you a window into some of their most interesting dishes. I hope you'll try to make them in your own kitchen, share them with family and friends, but if that soufflé just won't rise—you can always make a reservation. I know they'd be thrilled to see you. As far as my story goes, I'm just a journalist with an insatiable appetite for good food and the people behind it. If you have any questions about a restaurant or recipe, I hope you'll look me up—I'd love nothing more than to hear from you. Cheers!

4th & Swift

621 North Avenue NE
Atlanta, GA 30308
(678) 904-0160
4thandswift.com
Owner and Executive Chef: Jay Swift
Chef de Cuisine: Jeb Aldrich
Pastry Chef: Lauren Raymond

Plenty of restaurants profess a "farm-to-table" philosophy. Few actually walk the talk, but Jay Swift's modern American hot spot, 4th & Swift, surpasses the overused buzzword with their very own 3,000-square-foot farm to boot. Expect a bounty of turnips, beets greens, and tomatoes on the Baltimore native's menu, which Swift frames with his son Jeb Aldrich, a Johnson & Wales grad hailing from Charleston's Peninsula Grill and Atlanta's own Canoe and now-shuttered Joël. The father-son duo's refined comfort food (think, velvety sweet corn soup spiked with crab, crispy brussels sprouts salad, and melt-in-your-mouth roasted venison with spiced squash) is the perfect complement to the chic warehouse setting, which takes up residence in a former engine room situated in historic Old Fourth Ward, complete with warm pendant lamps, exposed brick walls, and high ceilings. Dine on the gorgeous patio during warmer months, when heirloom tomatoes appear on most tables, usually alongside Swift's legendary "Three Little Piggies," a plate full of pork done three ways. Inside or out, you can devise your meal from the Market Menu, which changes nightly, or opt for the five-course tasting menu. Whatever you do, finish with the sticky toffee pudding. And don't forget about Sunday brunch—Swift's house-made pork schnitzel and brisket hash put tired scrambled eggs to shame.

Summer Sweet Corn Soup with Lump Crab

(SERVES 6–8)

3 teaspoons vegetable oil

10 ears sweet yellow corn, kernels and juice removed, cob discarded

1 Vidalia onion, chopped

1 quart vegetable or chicken stock

1 cup heavy cream

Salt and white pepper to taste

1 ounce steamed lump or jumbo blue-crab meat

2 tablespoons fresh chopped chives

½ cup crème fraîche

Old Bay Seasoning to taste

Bring a large saucepan to medium-low heat and add oil. Add the corn and onion, sautéing for 4 minutes. Add half the stock and bring to a simmer. Remove the pan from heat and allow to cool.

Transfer most of the corn mixture to a blender, filling it about halfway. Add the heavy cream and carefully pulse on low speed to get started safely, then puree at high speed until velvety smooth. (*Note:* Add more stock if the mixture is too thick.) Strain mixture and return to saucepan.

Bring the soup to a simmer. Season with salt and pepper. Serve garnished with crabmeat, chives, crème fraîche, and a sprinkle of Old Bay.

North Georgia Apple & Crispy Brussels Sprout Salad

(SERVES 5)

4 cups apple cider
2 sprigs rosemary, leaves chopped
1 cup shelled, toasted pistachios, ground to coarse consistency
Pinch of fleur de sel
4 cups vegetable oil
25 brussels sprouts, stems removed, halved
2 tablespoons sherry vinegar
Salt and pepper to taste
1 cup crème fraîche
3 local apples (Ellijay Winesaps or Jonagolds preferred), peeled, cored, and cut into 1-inch slices

Place apple cider in a small pot over medium heat and reduce to syrup consistency, about 20 to 30 minutes. Cool and reserve.

In a medium bowl, combine the rosemary with pistachios and fleur de sel.

Heat the oil in a wide, deep pan or in a deep fryer to 350°F. Carefully add the sprouts to hot oil and fry until outside leaves begin to turn golden brown, about 4 minutes. Remove the sprouts from the oil and toss in a bowl with sherry vinegar, salt, and pepper.

Using a spoon, spread a line of crème fraîche on a plate to hold the sprouts in place. Liberally spread some of the reduced cider mixture on top of the crème fraîche. Place the sprouts in a line on top of the cider and crème fraîche. Top with the apples. Repeat to layer the salad. To finish, drizzle the remaining cider reduction over the top and sprinkle the pistachio-rosemary mixture liberally over the plate.

Aria

490 East Paces Ferry Road NE
Atlanta, GA 30305
(404) 233-7673
aria-atl.com
Managing Partner and Executive Chef: Gerry Klaskala
Chef de Cuisine: Brandon Hughes
Executive Pastry Chef: Kathryn King

Not many restaurants can claim 15 years of existence while simultaneously sitting at the top of nearly every "hot" restaurant list. But Aria, the brainchild of chef Gerry Klaskala (who also co-owns Canoe), isn't most restaurants. It's at once a special-occasion destination and everyday eatery. It's situated in the heart of ritzy Buckhead, yet decidedly down-to-earth. It's housed in a salvaged turn-of-the-century mansion, but juxtaposed

with modern art, metallic curtains, and a striking chandelier. "We're one foot in the past, one in the future," admits Klaskala, whose freestyle take on contemporary American cuisine has created a loyal following most chefs can only dream of. "I always wanted to have the perfect chef restaurant: 85 seats, the perfect kitchen with every toy and gizmo, a wine cellar, open for dinner only and closed on Sunday." Mission accomplished. Whether you sit in the sultry lounge, a sleek booth in the open dining room, or downstairs in the candlelit wine cellar, you're in for a treat. Particularly if you order one of Klaskala's celebrated slow-cooked dishes, like the Zinfandel-braised short ribs—the restaurant has sold more than 175,000 since opening—or the butter-braised lobster. And while a five-star review from the *Atlanta Journal-Constitution* (only five other restaurants have received this distinction) certainly helps, it's the consistency at Aria that solidifies the spot as one of Atlanta's best. "Every one of those short ribs was cooked by the same chef. Our fish cook, who's been here since day one, has cooked over 30,000 pounds of scallops. And our pastry chef, Kathryn King, has been here from the start, too. When you eat at Aria, you're in the hands of passionate people who truly care." Indeed.

Swordfish with Sweet & Sour Cipolline Onions

(SERVES 8 AS AN APPETIZER)

3 tablespoons extra-virgin olive oil, divided
2 cups cipolline onions, peeled
¼ cup whole peeled garlic cloves
4 sprigs fresh thyme
½ cup white balsamic vinegar
¼ cup honey
4 (8-ounce) swordfish steaks, cut ½ inch thick
Kosher salt to taste

Preheat oven to 350°F. Heat a heavy-bottomed sauté pan over medium heat. Add 2 tablespoons olive oil, cipolline onions, and garlic, and sauté for 7 to 8 minutes. Add the thyme and cook for an additional 2 minutes. Add the vinegar and honey, mix well, and bring to a simmer. Cover with foil and bake for 40 to 50 minutes, stirring occasionally. Remove the pan from the oven, cover, and allow to rest.

Preheat a charcoal grill to medium heat. Season the swordfish with salt and brush with the remaining1 tablespoon olive oil. Cook the swordfish until just barely cooked through, about 2 minutes, turn and then cook for 1 more minute.

Place the cooked swordfish on plates and top with the cipolline mixture. Serve.

Bacchanalia & Star Provisions

starprovisions.com
Owners and Executive Chefs: Anne Quatrano and Clifford Harrison

Abattoir

1170 Howell Mill Road NW
Atlanta, GA 30318
(404) 892-3335
Executive Chef: Hector Santiago

Bacchanalia and Quinones at Bacchanalia

1198 Howell Mill Road NW
Atlanta, GA 30318
(404) 365-0410
Executive Chef: David A. Carson
Chef de Cuisine: Matthew Adolfi
Pastry Chef: Carla Tomasko
General Manager: Frances Quatrano

Floataway Café

1123 Zonolite Road NE #15
Atlanta, GA 30306
(404) 892-1414
Executive Chef: Todd Immel

Star Provisions

1198 Howell Mill Road NW
Atlanta, GA 30318
(404) 365-0410
Executive Chef: Stiles Knight

It would be unthinkable to talk about Atlanta's food scene without mentioning Anne Quatrano, a trailblazer who—along with her husband, Clifford Harrison—opened one of the city's first chef-owned, independently operated, fine-dining restaurants back in 1993. That restaurant was Bacchanalia, and it changed Atlanta forever. It was (and still is) one of the city's only high-end restaurants offering multicourse tasting menus made from local, seasonal ingredients, and "Annie" was (and still is) the most pivotal force in Atlanta's farm-to-table movement. Today, the multiple James Beard award winner is the city's undisputed foodie heroine with five celebrated restaurants to her name, all of which "support local growers and ranchers into a vibrant and symbiotic relationship between farm and kitchens," says Quatrano, a California Culinary Academy grad. Indeed, 90 percent of the produce used on her menus comes from Annie's fifth-generation, 60-acre family farm, Summerland, in Cartersville, Georgia, where she and Harrison also live.

While Quatrano's Floataway Café is a true hidden gem—the romantic, airy spot is tucked away in a rather dubious industrial space—dishing up rustic, country French and Italian plates (the steak tartare and burrata with chimichurri are earth-shattering), meat-centric Abattoir—the name is French for "slaughterhouse," which is what the building used to be—is a Southern chophouse drawing on global influences in small plates like crunchy *chicharrónes*, smoky chorizo and octopus, and lamb liver fritters. For a more casual experience, head to Star Provisions, a 4,000-square-foot market-meets-gift-shop selling freshly baked bread and pastries (the sandwiches, particularly the shrimp po' boy and Reuben, are incredibly delicious), locally grown organic produce, and gourmet coffee alongside a butcher and seafood counter and trendy gifts like marble cheese trays and linen dish towels. Whichever spot you decide on, you're sure to find it in a location that is on its second or third life. "We believe to be truly sustainable you must also embrace sustainable building use, unlike the tear-down and rebuild mentality so often encountered." Where would Atlanta be without Annie? The answer: I'm sure nobody here ever wants to know.

Abattoir's Crispy Ceci Peas with Cumin Salt

(SERVES 6)

1 pound dry ceci peas (can substitute chickpeas)
2 bay leaves
1 sprig thyme
3 cloves garlic, peeled and crushed
1 tablespoon plus 1 teaspoon kosher salt, divided by use
1 quart peanut oil (can substitute canola oil)
1 teaspoon freshly ground cumin

Pick through the dry peas to remove any stones or other debris. Soak the peas in a 2-quart bowl of cold water that covers the peas by at least 4 inches. Keep the bowl in the refrigerator overnight. Drain the peas and rinse thoroughly.

Place the peas in a 4-quart saucepan, covering the peas with 4 inches of water over the top of the soaked peas. Add the bay leaves, thyme, and crushed garlic. Bring to a boil over medium-high heat and add 1 tablespoon salt. Reduce the heat to a very low simmer, skim off any foam that forms on the top of the water, and cook until the insides of the peas are creamy, about 2 hours. Remove from heat and drain. Cool the peas on sheet pan at room temperature. (*Note:* Once cooled, you can cover and store them in refrigerator.) Cool the peas on a paper towel–lined sheet pan at room temperature for an hour to air-dry them completely before frying.

Heat the peanut oil in an 8-quart stockpot to 350°F using a candy thermometer to measure temperature. With a spider or strainer, carefully lower the dry, cooked peas into the hot oil, 1 cup at a time. Fry the peas until golden brown, about 5 minutes. The skin of the peas should start to separate and crisp.

In a small bowl combine the fried peas with the remaining 1 teaspoon salt and ground cumin, tossing to coat. Serve immediately.

Bacchanalia's Crab Fritters

(SERVES 6–8)

For the mayonnaise:

1 egg yolk
1 whole egg
Juice of 1 lemon
½ tablespoon Dijon mustard
1 to 1½ cups peanut or canola oil
Salt and ground white pepper to taste

For the Thai pepper essence:

3 fresh Thai peppers, deseeded and chopped
1 fresh red chile pepper, deseeded and chopped
2 cloves garlic, roughly chopped
Juice of 3 limes
⅛ cup Thai fish sauce
½ cup maple syrup

For the vanilla oil:

1 vanilla bean, seeded
1 cup grapeseed oil

For the crab fritters:

1 pound fresh jumbo lump blue-crab meat, steamed not boiled, picked over for shells
½ cup homemade mayonnaise (recipe in instructions)
Dash of Tabasco Sauce
Salt to taste
1 cup panko (Japanese bread crumbs)
1 quart peanut oil
1 ripe, firm avocado
Assorted citrus supremes (1 orange, 1 grapefruit, 1 lime), peeled and sliced
½ cup Thai pepper essence (recipe in instructions)
Drizzle of vanilla oil (recipe in instructions)

To make the mayonnaise: Combine egg yolk, whole egg, lemon juice, and Dijon mustard in a food processor. Pulse until mixed well. Slowly drizzle in 1 to 1½ cups oil just until emulsified. Season with salt and ground white pepper to taste.

To make the Thai pepper essence: Combine Thai peppers with red chile pepper, garlic, lime juice, Thai fish sauce and maple syrup. Whisk to combine and refrigerate for at least 1 hour. Strain and reserve.

To make the vanilla oil: Combine the seeds of the vanilla bean with grapeseed oil and the vanilla bean itself in a glass container. Let stand for 1 hour at room temperature.

To make the crab fritters: In a large bowl, combine the picked crab with mayonnaise, Tabasco, and salt. Form into 6 to 8 balls and gently roll the balls in panko. In a heavy-bottomed stockpot, heat the peanut oil to 350°F. Fry the crab balls until golden brown, about 2 to 3 minutes per side. Serve in a bowl with sliced avocado and citrus supremes. Drizzle with Thai pepper essence and vanilla oil.

Floataway Café's Gateau Victoire

(Flourless Chocolate Cake)

(SERVES 8–10)

9 whole eggs
3 egg yolks
⅔ cup sugar
¾ cup hot espresso
1½ pounds chopped 66% bittersweet chocolate (Valrhona preferred)
1⅔ cup heavy whipping cream, whipped to soft peaks, plus additional for serving

Place the eggs, egg yolks, and sugar in the top of a double boiler. (*Note:* You can also place the ingredients in a clear glass bowl sitting over a saucepan of boiling water.) Whisk constantly until the temperature of mixture reaches 120°F. Transfer the mixture to a stand mixer fitted with a whisk attachment and whip on high speed for 30 minutes.

Preheat oven to 425°F.

In a large bowl, pour hot espresso over chopped chocolate, and stir until melted. Set aside.

In a large mixing bowl, gently fold the chocolate and whipped cream alternately into the whipped egg mixture.

Place the batter in a parchment-lined (bottom and sides) 9 x 13 x 2-inch baking pan. Place the baking pan in another larger pan filled with hot water. Bake for 90 minutes. Cool completely before serving. Serve with soft whipped cream.

(*Note:* You may refrigerate the cake overnight, but it must not be served cold. Leave out of refrigerator for at least 2 hours before serving.)

Star Provisions' Savory Tart

(SERVES 6)

1½ cups all-purpose flour
½ tablespoon salt
½ tablespoon black pepper
½ teaspoon sugar
4½ ounces cold unsalted butter, diced into 1-inch cubes
⅛ cup grated Parmesan cheese
⅛ cup ice-cold water
4 whole eggs
1 cup heavy cream
½ cup crumbled fresh goat cheese
½ pound roasted asparagus, cut into 2-inch pieces
½ teaspoon chopped chervil or tarragon
½ teaspoon chopped chives
¼ teaspoon salt
¼ teaspoon pepper

Mix dry ingredients (flour through sugar) in a bowl. Cut in the butter with a fork or pastry cutter. Add the Parmesan cheese and sprinkle in the ice water just enough to bring ingredients together. Keep cutting the dough with a fork or pastry cutter until pea-size pieces are formed.

Refrigerate the dough for at least 2 hours. Press the dough into ungreased 8-inch tart pan and then line with foil. (*Note:* Do not knead or roll the dough out as it will shrink and become dense if overworked.)

Preheat oven to 350°F. Fill the dough-lined tart pan with dry beans or pie weights and blind bake until golden brown, about 10 minutes. Remove the weights and bake 5 minutes longer. Set aside.

In a large bowl, mix together the eggs and heavy cream until incorporated but not frothy. Layer the goat cheese, asparagus, and fresh herbs into the partially baked tart shell and sprinkle with salt and pepper. Pour the custard over and bake in preheated 350°F oven until the top of the filling has puffed slightly and has a golden brown color, about 20 to 25 minutes. Let rest at least 5 minutes before serving.

Bocado

887 Howell Mill Road NW
Atlanta, GA 30318
(404) 815-1399
bocadoatlanta.com
Owner: Brian Lewis
Executive Chef: Adam Waller

The first time I dined at Bocado, the trendy Westside neighborhood hangout, was after an interview with chef Linton Hopkins; the mastermind behind Holeman + Finch's ultra-exclusive burger told me Bocado served *his* favorite burger in town (in his defense, they do use his bread company's bun). Hopkins was right. Bocado's pickle-heavy burger was easily the best I've had in Atlanta—melty American cheese cocooned two thin, charred patties made from a trio of house-ground meat (chuck, brisket, and short rib), resulting in a gloriously unctuous burger that has since made appearances in my dreams. But the real secret about Bocado isn't the burger (though they sell more than 600 every week)—it's chef Adam Waller (an Atlanta native previously of Sotto Sotto), whom I've come to call the "vegetable whisperer." The flavors Waller liberates from simple produce are revolutionary—in his hands, humble fava beans and lady peas are the highlight of the meal. Waller's seasonal small plates (don't miss the quinoa tossed with avocado, radish, and lime crème fraîche) change weekly based on what his farmers bring in, but favorites include the fiery roasted cauliflower hoagie and steak tartare in addictive horseradish crème, scooped up with mega-crunchy chips. All are best washed down with a cocktail—I'm partial to Lunar Park, an intoxicating amalgamation of rye, vermouth, and Gran Classico.

Steak Tartare

(SERVES 4)

For the tartare:

3 egg yolks
1½ teaspoons hot sauce
1 teaspoon Dijon mustard
1 tablespoon olive oil
2 tablespoons chopped capers
½ red onion, finely diced
¼ cup finely chopped parsley
1 tablespoon chopped chives
1 pound trimmed beef eye of round, chilled
Kosher salt and black pepper

For the herb salad:

1 cup parsley leaves
¼ cup finely sliced red onion
1 teaspoon chopped capers
1 tablespoon fresh lemon juice
¼ cup finely sliced scallions
2 tablespoons olive oil
Kosher salt and black pepper

For the horseradish crème:

2 tablespoons prepared horseradish
1 teaspoon fresh lemon juice
¼ cup sour cream
Kosher salt and black pepper

To make the tartare: In a medium bowl, combine the egg yolks, hot sauce, Dijon, olive oil, capers, red onion, parsley, and chives to make the dressing; mix well.

Mince the steak into very finely diced cubes. Add to the dressing and mix well. Season as needed with salt and pepper; chill in the refrigerator for 1 hour.

To make the herb salad: In a medium bowl, combine the parsley, onion, capers, lemon juice, scallions, and olive oil; season with salt and pepper.

To make the horseradish crème: In a small bowl, mix the horseradish with lemon juice and sour cream; season with salt and pepper.

To plate: Place the tartare on a chilled plate using a round pastry mold. Add a spoonful of the horseradish crème to the side and a spoonful of the herb salad to the other side. Serve with crostini.

Roasted Chicken Breast with Grits, Collards & White Wine Pan Sauce

(SERVES 4)

For the chicken:

4 skin-on, bone-in chicken breasts
Kosher salt and black pepper
1 tablespoon olive oil
¼ cup white wine
4 pickled cherry peppers, sliced
1 tablespoon unsalted butter

For the grits:

1 quart whole milk, plus more if needed
2 cups stone-ground white grits (Logan Turnpike Grits preferred)
2 tablespoons unsalted butter
Kosher salt and black pepper

For the collard greens:

2 tablespoons olive oil
½ pound bacon, cubed
1 large white onion, diced
2 cups red wine vinegar
½ cup sugar
1½ teaspoons chile flakes
1 bunch collard greens, washed and roughly chopped
2 quarts chicken stock
Kosher salt and black pepper

To make the chicken: Preheat the oven to 425°F. Season the chicken with salt and pepper on both sides. Heat the oil in a cast-iron skillet until smoking, about 1 minute. Add the chicken, skin side down, and let brown for 2 minutes; transfer skillet to preheated oven. Roast for 10 to 12 minutes, until the juices run clear. Remove the chicken and allow to rest.

Remove the excess oil from cast-iron skillet and place over high heat. Deglaze the pan with white wine, scraping up any browned bits. Add the peppers and reduce the liquid by half, about 2 to 3 minutes. Turn heat to low, stir in the butter until it's melted and incorporated, and season with salt and pepper.

To make the grits: In a medium saucepan over medium heat, bring the milk to a simmer; add the grits. On low heat, stir occasionally until the grits are creamy, about 40 minutes. Add additional milk as needed. Stir in the butter and season with salt and pepper to taste.

To make the collard greens: Combine the oil and cubed bacon in a large stockpot over medium-high heat; sauté 5 minutes or until the bacon is crispy but not burnt. Add the onion and cook until translucent and soft, about 2 to 3 minutes. Add the vinegar, sugar, and chile flakes and simmer for 2 minutes. Add the collards and cook until wilted, about 3 to 4 minutes. Add the chicken stock and simmer for 40 minutes, until the collards are tender. Season with salt and pepper.

To plate: Spoon the grits evenly onto four dinner plates. Place the collards on top of the grits alongside chicken breast. Spoon pan sauce over the chicken.

Black Rice Salad with Roasted Squash

(SERVES 4)

1 acorn or kabocha squash, diced
1½ cups olive oil
Kosher salt and black pepper to taste
2 cups toasted Brazil nuts
2 cups chopped cilantro
1 clove garlic, peeled
Zest of 2 limes
2 cups cooked black rice
1 cup golden raisins, soaked in equal parts vinegar and water, removed after 10 minutes
1 cup chopped toasted pistachios
4 cherry bell radishes, thinly sliced
2 shallots, thinly sliced
1 cup cilantro leaves
¼ cup thinly sliced scallions
3 tablespoons rice vinegar
1 tablespoon fresh lime juice
3 tablespoons olive oil

Roast squash with olive oil, salt, and pepper at 350°F degrees until tender, about 20 to 30 minutes.

In a food processor, place nuts, chopped cilantro, garlic, and lime zest. Add oil and pulse until you achieve a loose paste-like consistency. Season this "pesto" with salt and pepper.

In a large bowl, combine all remaining ingredients and season with salt and pepper. To serve, spoon pesto onto the bottom of a plate and top with black rice salad.

BoccaLupo

753 Edgewood Avenue NE
Atlanta, GA 30307
(404) 577-2332
boccalupoatl.com
Owner and Executive Chef: Bruce Logue
Chef de Cuisine: Ben Clayton

As I was writing this book, I spoke with dozens of Atlanta chefs about the city's food scene. Some have been here their whole lives, others are brand new. Some operated big, shiny restaurants, others small neighborhood joints. But unanimously, when asked who was making the biggest impact on Atlanta dining today, every single chef said Bruce Logue. Surprising when you consider the Georgia-born, Montana-raised chef not only got his start working on dude ranches but also cooks humble Italian-American soul food in a small Inman Park bungalow. But one bite of Logue's luxurious tagliatelle (it's made with 20 egg yolks!) or vibrant squid-ink spaghetti, a dish he brought over from his tenure at La Pietra Cucina (where he earned four stars from the *AJC*), and you understand. Logue's food, notably made-from-scratch, rolled, hand-cut, and extruded pasta, is fresh yet based on Old World techniques, a blissful union of his time cooking in Italy and working under Mario Batali. Fortunately, it's also insanely affordable—nothing on the menu exceeds $19, which might explain why it's so tough to snag a table at BoccaLupo. And in times when so many chefs would rather cook on TV than in their own restaurants, Logue is a true breath of fresh air. "I have cooked in this kitchen every single day we've been open. I don't ever want to be one of those chefs who carries a BlackBerry instead of a chef's knife."

Roman Fried Cauliflower with Mint & Meyer Lemon

(SERVES 4)

3 cups extra-virgin olive oil, divided
1 anchovy, chopped
1 clove garlic, chopped
1 head cauliflower, core and outer leaves removed, cut into bite-size florets
1 cup semolina flour
¼ cup torn mint leaves
½ cup whole parsley leaves
Juice of 1 Meyer lemon
1 teaspoon chile flakes
Salt and pepper
Zest of 1 Meyer lemon
¼ cup bread crumbs

Heat ¼ cup olive oil in a large sauté pan over medium heat. Add the chopped anchovy and garlic and cook until lightly browned, about 3 to 4 minutes. Allow to cool to room temperature; reserve.

Heat a medium pot over high heat with the remaining olive oil until it lightly smokes. (*Note:* You should have about 1 inch of olive oil in the pot.)

Dust the cauliflower in the semolina flour and fry in the oil until golden brown, about 2 minutes. (*Note:* You may need to fry in two batches.) Using a slotted spoon or spider, remove the cauliflower to paper towels; let drain and cool to room temperature.

Toss the cooled cauliflower in a large bowl with the torn mint, parsley, lemon juice, chile flakes, and the reserved anchovy-garlic oil. Season with salt and pepper to taste. Garnish with lemon zest and bread crumbs.

Bucatini with Smoked Bacon, Red Onion & Pecorino

(SERVES 4)

Salt
16 ounces bucatini
¼ cup extra-virgin olive oil, plus more as needed
1 cup diced smoked bacon (ends if possible)
1 clove garlic, sliced
1 red onion, sliced into half rings
1 (16-ounce) can San Marzano tomatoes, pureed
1 teaspoon thyme leaves
1 teaspoon chile flakes
Grated pecorino romano cheese
1 teaspoon chopped parsley

Bring a large pot of water to a boil and salt aggressively. Add the bucatini and cook until al dente, about 12 to 15 minutes. Drain.

Meanwhile, in a very large sauté pan or wide pot, add ¼ cup olive oil and bacon and cook over medium heat until the bacon has begun to render, about 4 minutes. Add the garlic and red onion and cook until the onion begins to brown and bacon is well crisped, about 5 minutes, sautéing regularly. Add the pureed tomatoes and raise the heat to high, cooking until the tomato has become dry and is frying in the bacon fat and oil, about 6 minutes. Add the thyme and chile flakes and reduce the heat to low. Add the cooked bucatini to the tomato sauce and toss to coat. Add in a little extra olive oil until shiny. Allow the pasta to stay in the sauce for 2 minutes before plating. Garnish with grated pecorino and chopped parsley.

Brick Store Pub

125 East Court Square
Decatur, GA 30030
(404) 687-0990
brickstorepub.com
Owners: Dave Blanchard, Mike Gallagher, and Tom Moore
Executive Chef: William Rian Tittle

It would be impossible to talk about beer in Atlanta without mentioning Decatur's Brick Store Pub, the holy grail of beer bars, home to a rotating reservoir of 21 drafts, 75 bottles, and even a second-floor 120-bottle-strong Belgian Bar, a temple of potent imports (read: ABV levels above 6 percent), including 8 rotating drafts. Fear not, oenophiles can enjoy this hoppy oasis, too—they also offer some two dozen varietals—and unlike your average pub, Brick Store (which has no TVs, no major domestic beers, and no neon signs) pays special attention to glassware, knowledgeable service, and food pairing, meaning the bites hold a candle to the brews. Don't leave without trying the traditional Brunswick stew and Bavarian soft pretzels. And, of course, no pub would be complete without fish-and-chips—chef William Rian Tittle's version employs fresh cod, hand dipped to order, alongside house-made remoulade sauce. Brick Store's success led owners Dave Blanchard, Mike Gallagher, and Tom Moore to open an unceremonious speakeasy, Leon's Full Service, in a converted gas station around the corner, and an oyster and cocktail bar, Kimball House, up the street. I can't wait to see what's next from these guys.

Hook's Three-Year Pimento Cheese

2½ pounds aged cheddar cheese (Hook's Three-Year Sharp preferred)
1 pound cheddar cheese (Tillamook preferred)
½ pound Monterey Jack cheese
2 cups grated Parmesan cheese
1 can pimientos, drained and diced
1 tablespoon ground cumin
¼ teaspoon cayenne pepper
½ teaspoon black pepper
½ cup mayonnaise

In a food processor fitted with the grater attachment, shred the first three cheeses. Transfer shredded cheese to a large serving bowl and add the grated parmesan and pimentos. Season with the cumin, cayenne pepper, and black pepper. Add the mayonnaise in small amounts until desired consistency is achieved. Add seasonings to taste and refrigerate until ready to use.

BRICK
BRICK

FIFA
WORLD CUP
ALL MATCHES
SHOWN LIVE!

Breweries

Twenty years ago, drinking beer in Atlanta was, to put it nicely, boring. Aside from the major domestics, the Big Peach had a big void. Today that picture looks much different, thanks to a handful of craft beer enthusiasts like Freddy Bensch, Kevin McNerney, and Greg Kelly, who revitalized the brew scene here when they opened SweetWater, 5 Seasons, and Atlanta Brewing Company (now Red Brick), respectively. Thanks to these trailblazers (and a ban lift that raised the legal ABV limit from 6 to 14 back in 2004), Atlanta is now home to a thriving craft-beer market chock-full of innovative ales, high-gravity beers, and one-of-a-kind sips. Herewith, a guide to eight of Atlanta's best breweries:

Eventide Brewing: This Grant Park brewery takes hands-on to a new level. The newcomer not only installed all their own equipment and did most of the build-out themselves, but it's also run by craftspeople who take pride in working with their hands (CEO Nathan Cowan is a fourth-generation engineer, and marketing guru Mathew Sweezey a third-generation woodworker). Brewmaster Geoffrey Williams is the only full-time employee in 2014 (Eventide's first year), but that hasn't stopped this inspired brewery from producing three killer ales. Don't miss their Kölsch-style ale, an approachable, light brew with notes of lemongrass and crisp hops. As we go to press, the brewery is not yet open for tours, but you can find their delicious beers in more than 100 bars, growler shops, and restaurants.

5 Seasons Brewing Company: Brewmasters Crawford Moran and Kevin McNerney, who hail from SweetWater and Colorado's Avery and Mammoth Brewing Companies, are in charge of nearly 70,000 gallons of beer at this Westside hangout. Each year, they release over 100 different beers, from crisp, refreshing Belgian Wits and bold IPAs to Farmhouse Ales made with local wildflower honey. The duo is constantly searching for new flavor combinations and works with local farmers—it's a give-and-take relationship, where 5 Seasons brews with their ingredients and, in turn, gives farmers the spent grain by-product for composting in their fields. You'll have to head to the Westside brewery for a taste; due to local laws, they aren't able to sell the beer elsewhere, but unlike most breweries, there's delicious food on offer, too.

Monday Night Brewing: Every Monday night since 2006, Jeff Heck, Joel Iverson, and Jonathan Baker have been brewing beer together (hence the name). No surprise that by 2011, the three former white-collar workers had quit their day jobs to pursue their passion: balanced, flavorful ales that pair well with food and are best drunk on the weeknights (the group's motto, naturally: "Weekends are overrated"). With four year-round beers and a rotating Black Tie Series, there's always something delicious to sip, though I'm personally smitten with Fu Manbrew, a bright and spicy Belgian-style Wit made with just a hint of ginger. Go for tours and tastings Monday, Thursday, and Saturday, or you can find their brews on the shelves at local retailers.

Red Brick Brewing: Formerly Atlanta Brewing Company (the oldest operational craft brewery in the Southeast), Red Brick, named for one of the original beers from 1993, makes two of Atlanta's best year-round beers: Hoplanta IPA, a citrus-forward American-style IPA, and Laughing Skull, a smooth, full-bodied amber ale. They're also responsible for four seasonals, including a chai tea–infused milk stout that's unlike anything you've likely tasted before. The innovative brewery's Brick Mason Series may be my favorite—I'm partial to the 3 Bagger, a rum-barrel-aged Belgian Tripel. Head to the brewery for tours and tastings Wednesday through Saturday—expect one-off beers on Wednesday, trivia on Thursday, and live music on the weekends. You can also find their beers at retailers throughout the South.

Second Self Beer Company: While working corporate nine-to-five jobs for four years, Jason Santamaria and Chris Doyle moonlighted as homebrewers, a fruitful attempt to create a second life for themselves, one that would eventually allow them to flee the rat race. With a goal of taking each imbiber on a journey with every sip, the duo has created four approachable, multilayered beers: Thai Wheat is a spicy, dry wheat beer with notes of lemongrass and ginger, while Red Hop Rye is full of hoppy citrus aromas balanced with malty caramel and honey. LIPA, a robust and aromatic IPA, is the perfect summer sipper—it's light and easy drinking. There's also a limited-release Saison chock-full of peppery, citrus notes. Find these brews at retail stores, in restaurants, or head to the brewery for tours and tastings, complete with food trucks.

SweetWater Brewing Company: Freddy Bensch and Kevin McNerney met as roommates at the University of Colorado, Boulder—the two took their first foray into the beer world washing kegs on the loading docks of a local brewery in exchange for free beer. They got a taste of something they liked and headed to the American Brewers Guild (brewing school), eventually brewing hoppy, aggressive ales for other breweries on the West Coast. By 1997, the boys had moved to Atlanta to open their own brewery, one of the city's first craft breweries, which now turns out 100,000 barrels a year. Named for a creek in a nearby park, SweetWater, which makes six year-round beers (their flagship 420 Extra Pale Ale is a mainstay in Atlanta), plus a handful of limited release and specials as part of their Dank Tank series (limited-time high-gravity beers), offers complimentary tours, and for just $10, you'll get a souvenir pint glass with six tasting tickets. It's one of my favorite ways to spend a Friday night.

Three Taverns Brewery: Brian Purcell started as a homebrewer, albeit one who won major competitions with his complex, Belgian-inspired all-grain recipes. So it was no surprise when this marketing pro turned brewmaster opened his own brewery. Named for a Roman resting place from the biblical book of Acts, Three Taverns is now an oasis where thirsty Atlantans can find rest, conversation, and, of course, good beer. Try the Single Intent, a lighter-bodied blonde ale, or A Night in

Brussels IPA, a Belgian-style American IPA with malts from Belgium. Twelve-dollar tastings and tours are available Friday and Saturday (bikers get $2 off!), though you can also find Three Taverns beers in local restaurants and retailers.

Wild Heaven Craft Beers: Named after the old R.E.M. song "Near Wild Heaven," this European-inspired brewery—it's run by Nick Purdy (founder of *Paste* magazine) and brewmaster Eric Johnson—launched in 2010, raising the level of beer in the South with an all-grain, no adjunct-sugar philosophy. Go for the Ode To Mercy, a rich, smooth brown ale made with coffee from Athens, Georgia's 1000 Faces, or White Blackbird, a pink-peppercorn-laced Belgian-style Saison. You can find them at most package stores and restaurants around town, or come in for tastings and tours.

Old Fourth Distillery

The year 2014 was a big one for Atlanta: countless restaurant openings, several James Beard nods, two new food-centric markets and the opening of the city's first distillery since Prohibition. Old Fourth Distillery, located in Atlanta's historic neighborhood of the same name, is the brainchild of brothers Jeff and Craig Moore (two techies who created BuyTough.com) and CARL, Germany's oldest still manufacturer renowned for its custom artisan distilling, mashing, and brewing equipment. The partnership resulted in Atlanta's first vodka—theirs is made with south Georgia cane sugar sourced from Dixie Crystal—and hopefully, down the road, gin and whiskey. The nearly 3,000-square-foot distillery plans to produce 60,000 bottles each year, and is open for tours and tastings. Bottoms up!

Buckhead Life Restaurant Group

buckheadrestaurants.com
Owner/President/CEO: I. Pano Karatassos

Atlanta Fish Market

265 Pharr Road NE
Atlanta, GA 30305
(404) 262-3165
Executive Chef: Robert Holley

Bistro Niko

3344 Peachtree Road
Atlanta, GA 30326
(404) 261-6456
Executive Chef: Gary Donlick

Buckhead Diner

3073 Piedmont Road NE
Atlanta, GA 30305
(404) 262-3336
Executive Chef: Charles Schwab

Chops Lobster Bar

70 West Paces Ferry Road NW
Atlanta, GA 30305
(404) 262-2675
Executive Chef: Ryan Delesandro

Corner Café

3070 Piedmont Road NE
Atlanta, GA 30305
(404) 240-1978
Executive Chef: Brendon Crapo

Kyma

3085 Piedmont Road NE
Atlanta, GA 30305
(404) 262-0702
Executive Chef: Pano I. Karatassos

Pricci

500 Pharr Road NE
Atlanta, GA 30305
(404) 237-2941
Executive Chef: Piero Premoli

Veni Vidi Vici

41 NW 14th Street
Atlanta, GA 30309
(404) 875-8424
Executive Chef: Jamie Adams

In 1979, Pano's & Paul's opened its doors in Buckhead. Nearly 40 years have passed, and I. Pano Karatassos is still the biggest name in the city's posh uptown neighborhood. Turns out, Pano's & Paul's was just the beginning for Karatassos, a Navy vet and Culinary Institute of America grad who went on to found the prominent Buckhead Life Restaurant Group, an eight-restaurant-strong ensemble that's been instrumental not only in pioneering Mediterranean cuisine in America but also with amplifying Atlanta's fine-dining touchstones.

Trailing on Pano's & Paul's success, Karatassos next opened Atlanta Fish Market, a neighborhood seafood sanctuary dishing up more than 100 fish flown in fresh daily, followed soon after by a private dining space called 103 West. In 1985, Karatassos channeled his inner Italian and opened Capriccio, which later became Pricci. Then came the legendary Buckhead Diner, a retro eatery full of nostalgia and classic Americana dishes. Next was Chops, Atlanta's iconic steak house complete with a Lobster Bar (the ultimate surf and turf). Veni Vidi Vici, a chic Italian trattoria, joined the group in 1993, followed by Buckhead Bread Company & Corner Café (a European-style bakery turning out 60-plus varieties of breads and rolls daily), Southwest-inspired Nava, and Asian-influenced Bluepointe (both of which have since closed, much to the heartache of locals).

The new millennium ushered in Kyma, a high-end seafood restaurant drawing on Greek and Mediterranean influences, and Bistro Niko, the chef's nod to Paris—the former of which brought Karatassos's son, Pano I. Karatassos, into the picture. Pano I. had been cooking at NYC's Jean-Georges and Le Bernardin, and at Napa Valley's The French Laundry (all of which are Michelin three-star restaurants) and returned home to man the stove at Kyma; he's since taken over as the group's corporate chef, as well.

No matter which restaurant you choose, one thing's for certain: Outstanding service, attention to detail, and consistently delicious food will all make appearances during your meal.

Atlanta Fish Market's Savannah Blue Crab & Sweet Pepper Bisque

(SERVES 12)

¾ pound (3 sticks) unsalted butter
2 large white onions, diced
6 large red bell peppers, diced
3 large green bell peppers, diced
1½ tablespoons minced garlic
1 tablespoon paprika
1 cup all-purpose flour
3½ cups sherry wine (Fairbanks California preferred), divided
2 quarts whole milk
2 cups heavy cream
6 chicken bouillon cubes
Salt and pepper to taste
1 pound jumbo lump crabmeat
12 ounces crab sticks

In an 8-quart sauce pot, melt the butter over medium heat. Add the onions, red and green peppers, garlic, and paprika. Cook until the vegetables are tender, about 8 to 10 minutes. Stir in the flour to form a roux and cook for 4 minutes, being careful not to burn the roux. Whisk in 3 cups sherry wine until smooth. Whisk in the milk, heavy cream, and bouillon cubes and cook until the soup begins to boil, about 10 minutes. Reduce the heat and season well with salt and pepper.

Puree the soup with an immersion blender. Add the crabmeat and crab sticks. Finish with the remaining ½ cup sherry wine. Serve.

Bistro Niko's Coq au Vin

(SERVES 4)

8 chicken legs, trimmed of excess fat
1 large onion, finely diced
2 large carrots, finely diced
2 stalks celery, finely diced
1 head garlic, unpeeled and cut in half
¼ cup chopped thyme
2 bay leaves
4 cups dry red wine
Salt and pepper to taste
4 tablespoons vegetable oil, divided
2 tablespoons tomato paste
3 tablespoons all-purpose flour
4 cups veal stock (can substitute beef stock)
1 cup pearl onions, peeled
4 ounces bacon, diced
1 pound button mushrooms, sliced and wiped free of dirt
3 tablespoons minced chives

In large pot, combine the chicken legs, onion, carrots, celery, garlic, thyme, and bay leaves. Cover with the red wine and lid and marinate overnight in the refrigerator. The next day, remove the chicken and strain the vegetables, reserving the marinade. Season the chicken with salt and pepper.

Preheat a dutch oven or large pot over high heat. Add 2 tablespoons vegetable oil and sauté the chicken legs until browned, about 8 to 10 minutes. Remove the chicken, set aside, and discard the oil. Add 2 tablespoons fresh oil and sauté the reserved vegetables from the marinade until lightly browned, about 10 minutes.

Preheat the oven to 350°F. Add the tomato paste and cook for 2 minutes. Add the flour and cook for 2 minutes. Add the reserved red wine from marinade, bring to a simmer, and stir with a wooden spoon to release browned bits from the bottom of the pot. Cook until wine is reduced by half, about 15 to 20 minutes. Add the veal stock and bring to a simmer. Return the chicken to the simmering liquid, cover with a lid, and cook until the chicken is tender, about 1½ hours.

While the chicken is cooking, blanch the pearl onions in simmering water for about 5 minutes. Set aside.

Cook the bacon in a sauté pan until lightly browned, about 8 minutes. Remove the bacon and set aside; add the mushrooms to the same pan, cooking until lightly browned, about 10 minutes. Add the blanched onions and cook until lightly browned, about 5 minutes.

Remove the chicken from the cooking liquid and strain the liquid into another pan, discarding the vegetables. Bring the cooking liquid to a simmer, skimming the sauce to remove excess fat. Simmer until the liquid is reduced by half, about 15 minutes, and return the chicken to the pot. Add the browned mushrooms, pearl onions, and bacon and simmer for 20 minutes. Garnish with minced chives and serve.

Buckhead Diner's Collard Greens & Ham Soup

(SERVES 4)

For the ham:

1 carrot, roughly chopped
½ white onion, diced
2 ribs celery, roughly chopped
2 tablespoons canola oil
2 quarts pork stock (can substitute chicken stock)
1 smoked ham shank (Patak preferred)
2 bay leaves
4 sprigs thyme
4 black peppercorns

For the collards:

2 ribs celery, finely diced
½ white onion, finely diced
2 cloves garlic, chopped
2 tablespoons (¼ stick) unsalted butter
2 tablespoons all-purpose flour
1½ quarts reserved ham stock
1 bunch collard greens, ribs removed, leaves chopped
½ cup heavy cream
1 tablespoon malt vinegar
Hot sauce to taste (Tabasco preferred)
1 teaspoon red pepper flakes
Kosher salt to taste

To make the ham: A day before serving, in a small pot over medium heat, sauté the carrot, onion, and celery in the canola oil. Add the next five ingredients (stock through peppercorns), cover, and simmer over very low heat until the shank is falling off the bone, about 6 hours. Remove the pot from heat and cool to room temperature before placing the entire pot covered in the refrigerator overnight. The next day, carefully remove the shank, reserving the meat and discarding the bone. Heat the stock over medium heat and strain, reserving the liquid.

To make the collards: In a 12-quart pot, sweat the celery, onion, and garlic in butter over medium heat until tender and translucent, about 5 to 10 minutes. Whisk in the flour to make a roux. Add the reserved ham stock and collard greens and bring to a simmer over low heat until the collards become tender, about 10 minutes. Add the ham, heavy cream, malt vinegar, hot sauce, red pepper flakes, and salt. Taste and adjust seasoning as needed. Serve.

Corner Café's Smoked Salmon Benedict

(SERVES 4)

For the hollandaise:

3 egg yolks
1 tablespoon lemon juice
½ tablespoon Worcestershire sauce
½ tablespoon Tabasco Sauce
½ teaspoon salt
10 teaspoons melted unsalted butter
2 tablespoons sour cream
2 tablespoons chopped chives

For the fried onions:

1 Vidalia onion, shaved on a mandoline
1 cup milk
1 cup all-purpose flour
¼ cup cornstarch
1½ teaspoons kosher salt
½ teaspoon ground white pepper
1 quart vegetable oil for frying

For the potato blini:

1½ pounds Idaho potatoes, peeled, boiled until just soft, drained, and riced
⅓ cup cornstarch
3 egg yolks
Salt and white pepper to taste
1½ cups heavy cream, warmed
3 egg whites, whipped into soft peaks

For plating:

10 ounces smoked salmon
4 poached eggs

To make the hollandaise: Using a blender, combine first five ingredients (egg yolks through salt); pulse to combine. While the blender is on low, add the melted butter in a thin stream to create an emulsion. Fold in the sour cream and chives. Set aside at room temperature.

To make the fried onions: Soak the shaved onions in milk for 5 minutes. Meanwhile, in a shallow dish, combine the next four ingredients (flour through white pepper). Remove the onions from the milk and toss in the flour mixture, coating the onions thoroughly.

In a heavy-bottomed pot or deep fryer, heat the oil to 350°F. Carefully add the onions in batches to the hot oil and fry until golden brown, about 4 to 6 minutes. Remove the onions from the oil and drain on paper towels.

To make the potato blini: In a large bowl, combine the riced potatoes, cornstarch, egg yolks, salt, and white pepper; mix well. Add one-third of the warmed heavy cream to temper the mixture. Fold in the egg whites, adjusting consistency with additional heavy cream until a pancake-like batter is formed.

Heat a griddle pan to medium-high and spray with cooking spray. Place four silver-dollar-size portions of batter on the griddle and cook until bubbles start to appear, about 2 to 3 minutes. Flip and cook until golden brown and firm, about 1 to 2 minutes. Repeat with remaining batter.

To plate: Place 2 blinis on each of four plates. Top each plate with 2½ ounces smoked salmon and 1 poached egg. Finish with the hollandaise sauce and fried onions.

Kyma's Grilled Whole Sea Bass "Lavraki" with Lemon Vinaigrette & Wild Greens

(SERVES 4)

For the lemon vinaigrette:

6 saffron threads
½ tablespoon dry mustard
½ cup fresh lemon juice
½ cup vegetable oil
½ cup extra-virgin olive oil (Greek preferred)
½ tablespoon salt
½ tablespoon white pepper

For the fish:

2 (1- to 2-pound) whole striped bass, scaled, gutted, and scored along the backbone
Salt and pepper to taste

For the wild greens:

½ cup olive oil
2 pounds dandelion greens, cleaned and roughly chopped
Salt and pepper to taste
4 lemons, juiced
¼ cup extra-virgin olive oil

For plating:

½ cup chopped fresh parsley
4 tablespoons capers
4 lemon wedges

To make the lemon vinaigrette: Place the saffron, dry mustard, and lemon juice in a blender and puree on high speed for 5 minutes. Slowly pour in the oils and puree on high speed until emulsified, about 3 minutes. Season with salt and pepper. Set aside 1 cup for basting the fish; the remaining cup is for sauce.

To make the fish: Preheat a grill to medium (roughly 375°F), lightly oiling the grates to prevent the fish from sticking. Meanwhile, season the fish with the salt, pepper, and 1 cup lemon vinaigrette. Place the fish into a skada (a grilling rack for whole fish) that has been liberally sprayed with oil. Place the fish on the grill and cook both sides of the fillet for 6 to 8 minutes on each side. (*Note:* You can test for doneness by inserting a toothpick into the flesh closest to the head, removing it, and touching it to your lip. It should feel warm but not hot.)

Remove the fish to a cutting board and let rest for 5 minutes. Remove the head and tail of the fish. Then remove each fillet and the backbone of the fish. Remove the small pin bones with a pair of fish tweezers.

To make the wild greens: Heat a large sauté pan over medium heat and add the olive oil. Once the oil just begins to smoke, add the greens and allow them to wilt while you stir and toss, about 3 minutes. Remove the sauté pan from heat and season with the salt, pepper, lemon juice, and extra-virgin olive oil.

To plate: Place the fish fillets onto a platter with the head and the tail. Garnish the fish with chopped parsley, capers, lemon wedges, and remaining lemon vinaigrette. Serve with braised greens.

Pricci's Tuna Crudo

(SERVES 4)

12 ounces center-cut, grade A tuna loin, cut into 1½-inch-thick logs
Sea salt and pepper to taste
4 tablespoons finely chopped chives
4 tablespoons finely chopped parsley
1 tablespoon extra-virgin olive oil
2 tablespoons tangerine juice (can substitute orange or grapefruit juice)
4 tablespoons canola oil
1 tablespoon minced shallot
1 tablespoon Dijon mustard
12 tablespoons kale, finely shaved
4 tablespoons fennel, finely shaved
4 tablespoons tangerine segments

Season the tuna logs with salt and pepper. Rub the logs into the chives and parsley. In a hot skillet over medium heat, heat olive oil. Sear the tuna until rare, only a few seconds per side. Set the tuna aside in the refrigerator.

In a mixing bowl, whisk together the tangerine juice, canola oil, shallot, Dijon, and salt and pepper to taste. Pour 4 tablespoons vinaigrette into a bowl filled with the kale and fennel, reserving the rest. Set both aside.

To serve, evenly divide the kale and fennel mixture among four plates. Add tuna to each. Dress with sea salt and the remaining vinaigrette. Garnish with the tangerine segments and serve.

Veni Vidi Vici Strawberry Pizza

(SERVES 6)

4 ounces Stracchino cheese (can substitute Brie cheese with rind removed)
8 ounces finely grated fontina cheese
12 ounces mascarpone
1 (17.3-ounce) box frozen puff pastry, thawed
Flour for dusting
Confectioners' sugar for dusting
1 (12-ounce) jar strawberry jam
20 fresh strawberries, washed, hulled, and sliced crosswise
5 teaspoons raw sugar
Aged balsamic vinegar for drizzling
½ pint heavy cream, whipped
Mint leaves for garnish

Mix together the three cheeses and put into a pastry bag. Set aside.

Preheat the oven to 350°F.

Using a rolling pin, roll the puff pastry into 6 thin rounds about 8 inches across. (*Note:* Use a little flour and confectioners' sugar to keep the dough from sticking.) Line two cookie sheets with parchment paper and lay the dough rounds on top of the paper, making sure they don't touch. Cover the dough with another sheet of parchment paper and place an identical cookie sheet on top. Bake until golden, about 10 minutes. Remove the top cookie sheet just before the crusts are done to check the color. Cool at room temperature.

Spread the strawberry jam on each crust. Pipe three or four stripes of the cheese mixture over the jam. Lay the strawberry slices on top and sprinkle with the raw sugar. Bake again until the cheese is melted and the edges are slightly brown, about 5 to 8 minutes.

Just before serving, drizzle the pie with the balsamic vinegar and garnish with a dollop whipped cream and mint leaves. Serve hot.

Cakes & Ale

155 Sycamore Street
Decatur, GA 30030
(404) 377-7994
cakesandalerestaurant.com
Owner and Executive Chef: Billy Allin

You know those restaurants that are just small enough to feel intimate and welcoming but just large enough to feel convivial and lively? Those restaurants that are so remarkable in their simplicity that with every bite you have to remind yourself that it's just peaches or just trout or just cauliflower? That's Cakes & Ale. Only it's not just peaches or trout or cauliflower. More thought and honesty go into chef-owner Billy Allin's food than most restaurants in Atlanta (heck, in the entire country!). No surprise considering the South Carolina–raised chef trained under Alice Waters, the pioneer of the farm-to-table movement, and Scott Peacock of Atlanta's own Watershed. "I tried to model Cakes & Ale after Chez Panisse," admits Allin, a California Culinary Academy alum who teamed up with his wife, Kristin, to open Cakes & Ale. "There's a purpose to every dish. We're trying to capture a moment, to get into your soul, to change the way people eat." So most plates are vegetable heavy, or at least laced with greens, rather than overloaded with starch. Everything is made to order by hand, primarily from sustainably sourced, organic, Georgia-grown ingredients, sometimes even ones cultivated in the James Beard award semifinalist's veggie garden out back. "There's no cutting corners here—farmers have even told me I'm hard to work with because I send anything back if the quality isn't there," says Allin, whose Italian-leaning menu changes constantly to make room for seasonal ingredients. If you're lucky, the addictive gnocchi cloaked in lamb ragù will make an appearance, hopefully alongside briny clams tossed with fava beans and fennel, and buttery burrata draped with whatever's in season that week. Be sure to stop at Allin's cafe next door, where gorgeous white marble counters dispense decadent pastries, sandwiches, and coffee.

Sweet & Sour Butternut Squash

(SERVES 6)

1 small, brightly colored butternut squash (approximately 1½ pounds)
3 tablespoon extra-virgin olive oil
¼ cup cider vinegar
3 tablespoons honey (preferably wildflower or chestnut)
Pinch of chile flakes
1 clove garlic, minced
Salt to taste
6 small mint leaves for garnish

Cut the neck off the squash, slicing off the stem end. Set the neck upright and cut off the skin. Repeat with the body of the squash, cutting off the stem end and then the skin. Cut the body in half and remove the seeds and membranes. Slice the neck and the two halves of the body into ½-inch crosswise slices.

Heat the olive oil in a large sauté pan over medium heat until the oil slides easily across the pan. Add the squash in one layer to the pan and do not stir. (*Note:* If your pan isn't large enough to place all the squash slices in one layer, sauté in batches). After 2 minutes, give the pan a gentle shake and leave until one side of the slice is brown, about 4 to 5 minutes. Turn with a fork and cook until the other side is brown and the squash is just tender but not falling apart, about 3 to 4 minutes.

Add vinegar, honey, chile flakes, garlic, and salt, stirring to coat squash with the sauce. Let the mixture cook down until it coats the squash but is still a little loose, about 1 to 2 minutes. Serve immediately, garnished with mint.

Fresh Sweet Strawberries with Shaved Parmigiano Reggiano

(SERVES 6)

1 pint spring strawberries, hulled
Parmigiano Reggiano, shaved into 12 to 14 thin strips with a vegetable peeler
Black pepper to taste
1 tablespoon extra-virgin olive oil (buttery Ligurian oil preferred)

Cut strawberries into thin slices and arrange on a platter. Top with Parmigiano Reggiano and black pepper to taste and drizzle with olive oil. Serve.

New Crop Potato, Apple & Fennel Salad

(SERVES 4–6)

1 shallot, minced
2 tablespoons cider vinegar
Salt
½ pound jewel yams, peeled and cut into ½-inch dice
¼ pound fingerling potatoes, peeled and cut into ½-inch dice
¼ pound Peruvian blue potatoes, peeled and cut into ½-inch dice
½ cup mayonnaise (homemade preferred)
1 teaspoon Dijon mustard
1 tablespoon capers, soaked in water for 15 minutes and drained
1 tablespoon chopped parsley
Pepper to taste
1 Gala apple, peeled, cored, and cut into ½-inch dice
1 long, slender fennel bulb, halved, cored, and thinly sliced across the grain

In a small bowl, combine the minced shallot with the cider vinegar and a pinch of salt; mix well and set aside.

Place three small pots on the stove. Fill each pot with water to cover potatoes by 2 inches and season with 1 teaspoon of salt. Put each type of potato (yams, fingerling, and blue) in a separate pot. Turn on the stove and bring each pot to a simmer over medium heat. Cook the potatoes until each is just tender, about 6 to 8 minutes. Drain the potatoes and spread them on a sheet tray to cool slightly.

In a large bowl, combine the mayonnaise, shallot-vinegar mixture, mustard, capers, parsley, and pepper to taste. Gently fold in the potatoes, apples, and fennel. Serve at room temperature.

Community Farmers Markets

With a mission to cultivate farmers' markets for lasting sustainability and meaningful neighborhood impact, Community Farmers Markets, a nonprofit organization, has built stronger local food systems throughout Atlanta with their four markets:

Two Decatur Farmers Markets (open Wednesday and Saturday from April through December)

East Atlanta Village Farmers Market (open every Thursday evening from April through December)

Grant Park Farmers Market (open every Sunday from April through December)

Though all four markets are unique in their own right, there are some common denominators. All provide fresh, nutritious food options (think organic, free-range, non-GMO products naturally grown within 10 miles of the city, alongside homemade desserts, bath products, and pet supplies). They all also host playful environments where people from all backgrounds gather each week to celebrate community with amazing food, family-friendly activities, and live music. And they all participate in the "Double Your Dollars" program in partnership with Wholesome Wave Georgia, which doubles SNAP (Supplemental Nutrition Assistance Program) benefit recipients' EBT (electronic benefit transfer) card values if used at the market, and the "My Market Club" program with Georgia Organics, which gives new customers three-tiered incentives to continue visiting the market, like $5 to spend on any food at market. Money you can feel great about spending.

Canoe

4199 Paces Ferry Road SE
Atlanta, GA 30339
(770) 432-2663
canoeatl.com
Owners: George McKerrow, Ron San Martin, and Gerry Klaskala
Executive Chef: Matthew Basford
Wine Director: Matt Bradford
Pastry Chef: Sarah Koob

In an age where new restaurants open (and often shutter) on a daily basis and diners are infatuated with the next "it" spot, there's something heartening about restaurants that have endured. One such place is Canoe, an Atlanta institution since 1995, renowned for its view—the restaurant sits on the banks of the Chattahoochee River, complete

with tree-lined, pebbled walkways and verdant gardens. "Canoe is everyone's favorite modern American cuisine—there's something for everyone on the menu," says executive chef and Australia-native Matthew Basford. "Rather than pigeonhole ourselves into one type of cuisine, we just strive for our food to taste great. You can't argue with delicious." Though Canoe's menu changes seasonally, you're all but guaranteed its signature house-smoked salmon and the slow-roasted Carolina rabbit—the restaurant goes through 110 rabbits a week (that's *a lot* of rabbit!). While these dishes might be the restaurant's bedrocks, and for good reason, Basford, who brings a Pan-Asian touch to the menu, is equally proud of his flash-fried calamari tossed in sesame chile sauce and grilled octopus with smoky chorizo. Whatever you choose, expect comfort, plain and simple. "You can show up in shorts and a T-shirt for a relaxing dinner, and you'll get the same great service and food as the guy in a suit trying to impress his boss. It's the true Southern experience: great service, good food, and a view." The 300-plus wine list—40 of which are available by the glass—doesn't hurt either.

Edamame Hummus

(SERVES 4)

1 pound frozen shelled edamame
Salt
¼ cup tahini
¼ cup water
Juice of 1 lemon
Juice of 1 lime
3 cloves roasted garlic
1 raw garlic clove, crushed
1 tablespoon rice vinegar
1 tablespoon soy sauce
3 tablespoons extra-virgin olive oil
Cilantro puree (see Note)

In a large saucepan over high heat, boil the edamame in salted water until super soft, about 10 to 15 minutes.

Add the cooked edamame to a food processor along with the next eight ingredients (tahini through soy sauce). Puree until smooth. With the motor running, slowly drizzle in the olive oil and mix until absorbed. Transfer mixture to a serving dish and chill in the refrigerator for 2 hours.

To finish, place the hummus base mixture back into food processor and turn on. Slowly add cilantro puree until the hummus turns light green. Transfer the hummus to a serving bowl and chill in the refrigerator, covered with plastic wrap, until ready to serve. Enjoy with grilled sourdough or flatbread.

(*Note:* To make cilantro puree, blanch 2 bunches cilantro. Chill immediately. Once chilled, puree with a few ice cubes until smooth.)

Sweet Potato & Clam Chowder

(SERVES 8–10)

1 yellow onion, peeled and diced
3 ounces (¾ stick) butter
¼ pound applewood-smoked bacon, diced
2 cloves garlic, minced
6 tablespoons flour
16 tablespoons white wine
1 Idaho potato, peeled and diced
4 large sweet potatoes, peeled and chopped
½ gallon chicken stock
Salt and pepper to taste
½ quart heavy cream
12 tablespoons crème fraîche, plus more for garnish
¼ pound clams, shelled, with juice reserved
1¼ pounds cooked lobster meat (tail and claw), diced, for garnish
4 tablespoons chili oil, for garnish

In a large soup pot over medium heat, sauté the onions with butter and bacon until the onions are translucent, about 5 minutes. Add the garlic and cook for 1 minute more. Add the flour; mix until well combined and cook for 3 minutes to make a roux. Add the white wine and bring to simmer. Once simmering, add the potato, sweet potato, chicken stock, and season with salt and pepper to taste. Cook until the sweet potato is soft, about 20 minutes. Add the heavy cream and bring to a boil. Remove from the heat and allow to cool.

Add the soup to a blender, pureeing on low in batches, increasing speed to high for 30 seconds once the mixture is moving. (*Note:* Do not fill the blender above halfway.) Return the pureed soup to the soup pot; add crème fraîche and season with salt and pepper.

When ready to serve, add the clams and clam juice and bring the soup back to a boil. Garnish with lobster meat, a dollop of crème fraîche, and a drizzle of chili oil.

Chinese BBQ Quail with Southern Collards

(SERVES 8)

- 1 (8.5-ounce) jar char sui (Chinese BBQ sauce)
- 2 cups honey
- 1 star anise
- ¼ stick cinnamon
- ½ cup orange juice
- 8 plantation quail, semi-boned with only wing and leg bones remaining
- 2 ounces (½ stick) unsalted butter
- ½ white onion, diced
- 1 clove garlic, crushed
- ½ pound applewood-smoked bacon (Neuskey's preferred)
- ¼ jalapeño, finely diced
- ½ cup apple cider vinegar
- 1 cup apple cider
- 1½ cups chicken stock, divided
- 1 bunch collards, stemmed and roughly chopped
- Salt and pepper to taste
- ¼ cup light brown sugar
- 1 pound Spanish peanuts
- ½ (14-ounce) can coconut milk
- 3 tablespoon hoisin sauce

In a large stainless steel mixing bowl, mix the char sui with the honey, star anise, cinnamon, and orange juice to combine. Add the quail, cover, and marinate overnight in the refrigerator. Remove from refrigerator 2 hours before ready to use. Place the quail on a grill preheated to low heat; grill 5 minutes per side for medium-rare. Cut each quail down the middle; reserve.

Meanwhile, in a large sauté pan over medium heat, melt the butter and add the onion, garlic, bacon, and jalapeño. Sauté for 5 minutes. Add the cider vinegar and cook until liquid is reduced by half, about 10 to 15 minutes. Add the apple cider and 8 ounces chicken stock, bring to a simmer, and add the collards. Cook for 1 hour. Season with salt, pepper, and brown sugar to taste. (*Note:* The collards should only have a slight acidic taste after a slightly sweet start.)

Place the peanuts, remaining 4 ounces chicken stock, and coconut milk in a saucepan over medium heat. Let simmer until the peanuts become soft, about 10 minutes. Remove from heat and allow to cool. Once cooled, transfer the peanut mixture to a blender and puree until smooth, starting on low speed and gradually increasing to high to prevent spills. Add the hoisin and season with salt and pepper to taste.

To serve, divide the peanut puree between eight plates. Top with the collards and the quail.

Castellucci Hospitality Group

castelluccihg.com
Owner: Federico Castellucci

Cooks & Soldiers

691 14th Street NW
Atlanta, Georgia 30318
(770) 817-8000
cooksandsoldiers.com
Executive Chef: Landon Thompson

Double Zero Napoletana

5825 Roswell Road
Atlanta, GA 30328
(404) 991-3666
doublezeroatl.com
Executive Chef: Edwin Molina

Sugo

10305 Medlock Bridge Road
Johns Creek, GA 30097
(770) 817-8000
sugorestaurant.com
Executive Chef: Ricardo Soto

The Iberian Pig

121 Sycamore Street
Decatur, GA 30030
(404) 371-8800
theiberianpigatl.com
Co-Owner and Executive Chef: Chad Crete

When I started writing about food back in 2008, my first assignment was covering the opening of a playful Spanish tapas bar setting up shop in Decatur called The Iberian Pig. I was blown away—not only was the food superlative (I'm mad about the pork cheek tacos and foie gras french toast), the beverage program unique (there are 30-odd sherries on the list), and the setting inspired (original brick from the building's previous life as a 1940s shoe store peeks through the walls), but the owner, Federico (Fred) Castellucci, was just 24 years old. Talk about feeling inadequate. But one bite of *jamón ibérico* and all my worries vanished. As it turns out, this wasn't Fred's first *corrida*; his father, officially of the same name, though most know him as Mr. C, opened Sugo (an Italy-meets-Greece Old World restaurant in Roswell) back in 2003. Together they grew the concept into four locations before Fred opened The Iberian Pig, and subsequently Double Zero Napoletana, a contemporary southern Italian eatery, and Cooks & Soldiers, a Basque-inspired restaurant on the burgeoning Westside. Each is the perfect spot for delicious meals full of community and merriment. My kind of eating.

Cooks & Soldiers' Cana de Cabra Pintxo

(SERVES 8)

For the shallot jam:

½ tablespoon olive oil
1 cup shallots, thinly sliced
⅛ cup sherry (Pedro Ximenez preferred)
2 tablespoons turbinado sugar
3 tablespoons sherry vinegar

For the Cana de Cabra pintxo:

2 medium green bell peppers
1 tablespoon plus 1 teaspoon extra-virgin olive oil, divided
Salt and pepper to taste
1 French baguette, sliced on the bias into ¼ x 3-inch pieces
8 ounces Cana de Cabra cheese (can substitute Brie cheese)
1 cup roasted tomatoes, sliced (see Sugo's Meatballs recipe below; can substitute sun-dried tomatoes packed in olive oil)
1 cup shallot jam (recipe in instructions)
¼ cup candied pistachios

To make the shallot jam: Place a medium saucepan over medium heat. Add olive oil and shallots. Cook until translucent, about 3 to 4 minutes. Add sherry and turbinado sugar and reduce until a syrup consistency is achieved, about 10 minutes. Remove the mixture from heat and add sherry vinegar, stirring to combine. Set aside.

To make the Cana de Cabra pintxo: Season the green bell peppers with 1 tablespoon olive oil and salt and pepper. Place the peppers directly over an open flame of a gas stove (or char on an open grill) until the skin is completely charred, about 3 to 4 minutes per side. Set the peppers in a mixing bowl and wrap with plastic wrap to trap the heat; let sit for 10 minutes. Remove the peppers from the bowl, and slide the skin off the peppers. Discard the seeds and slice the peppers into ¼-inch strips. Set aside.

Preheat the oven to 350°F. Season the baguette slices with the remaining teaspoon olive oil and salt and pepper. Place on a baking sheet and toast the bread until golden brown, about 8 minutes.

Top each toasted bread slice with ½-ounce slices of cheese, a strip of the roasted bell pepper, and a small slice of roasted tomato. Finish with 1 teaspoon shallot jam and garnish with the candied pistachios. Hold at room temperature for 15 to 30 minutes. Serve.

Double Zero Napoletana's Butternut Squash Fritters

(SERVES 4–6)

For the caramelized onion aioli:

1 medium onion, julienned
2 tablespoosn olive oil
2 cups mayonnaise

For the lemon honey:

1 cup clover honey
Juice of 2 lemons

For the fritters:

⅔ cup all-purpose flour
1 teaspoon baking powder
1 tablespoon kosher salt, plus more to taste
1 cup soda water
1½ tablespoons clover honey
3 cups butternut squash, peeled and grated
1½ quarts vegetable oil
1 cup caramelized onion aioli (recipe in instructions)
½ cup lemon honey (recipe in instructions)

To make the aioli: Cook onion and olive oil in a large sauté pan over medium-low heat until caramelized, about 40 minutes. Finely dice the caramelized onions and combine with mayonnaise, mixing well. Set aside.

To make the lemon honey: Combine clover honey with lemon juice in a mixing bowl, stirring to combine. Set aside.

To make the fritters: In a large mixing bowl, combine the flour, baking powder, and 1 tablespoon kosher salt. Slowly stir in the soda water until well incorporated. Add the honey and mix thoroughly. Fold in the grated butternut squash until fully incorporated. (*Note:* The fritter batter will hold, refrigerated in an airtight container, for up to 3 days.)

Heat the oil in a heavy-bottomed pot or a deep fryer until a candy thermometer registers 350°F. Using a 2-ounce ice scream scoop, drop the fritter batter into the hot oil, eight at a time to avoid overcrowding the fryer. Fry until the fritters are golden brown and completely cooked through, turning halfway through, about 5 to 6 minutes. Drain on a pan lined with paper towels and season with kosher salt. Dress each fritter with the caramelized onion aioli and lemon honey. Serve.

Sugo's Meatballs

(SERVES 10)

For the roasted tomatoes:

12 Roma tomatoes, halved lengthwise
1 tablespoon dried oregano
1 tablespoon Italian seasoning
2 tablespoons chopped garlic
½ tablespoon coarse salt (kosher or Maldon sea salt preferred)
½ tablespoon cracked black pepper
¼ cup extra-virgin olive oil

For the caramelized onions:

1 pound yellow onions, sliced
2 tablespoons honey
1 tablespoon Spanish paprika
1 tablespoon powdered chicken base
½ cup aged balsamic vinegar
2 cups canola oil

For the meatballs:

5 pounds wild boar sausage, skins removed (can substitute mild Italian sausage)
3 eggs
1 cup chopped dates
1 cup Pecorino Romano cheese
¾ cup bread crumbs
2 tablespoons olive oil, plus more for serving

To make the roasted tomatoes: Preheat oven to 225°F. Place the tomatoes in a large mixing bowl with the oregano, Italian seasoning, garlic, salt, and pepper. Mix until evenly coated. Place the tomatoes, cut side down, in a baking dish fitted with a wire rack. Bake for 2 hours. Remove the tomatoes from the rack and place them in a container with enough olive oil to slightly cover the tomatoes. Leave at room temperature.

To make the caramelized onions: Preheat the oven to 275°F. Place the onions in a bowl with the remaining ingredients. Toss until evenly coated. Place the onions in a baking dish and cover with aluminum foil. Bake for 2½ hours. Remove the baking dish and foil and let the onions cool. Set aside.

To make the meatballs: Preheat the oven to 375°F. Place the sausage in a large mixing bowl. Crack the eggs into a separate container and inspect for shells; add to the sausage. Add the dates and cheese and mix well with your hands. Gradually add the bread crumbs. Using a large ice cream scoop, mold the mixture into balls. Place the meatballs on a full sheet pan with 1 ounce of olive oil on the bottom. Bake for 25 minutes.

Serve with your favorite tomato sauce, some Pecorino Romano cheese, fresh basil, and a drizzle of extra-virgin olive oil.

The Iberian Pig's Bacon-Wrapped Dates

(SERVES 4–6)

1 cup Manchego cheese, finely chopped
1 cup toasted walnut pieces
1 pound Medjool dates, pits removed
1 pound applewood-smoked bacon, cut into 3-inch slices
Vegetable oil for frying
½ cup balsamic glaze (can be bought at specialty stores or made by reducing ¾ cup balsamic vinegar and 1½ cups fine granulated sugar)

In a large bowl, combine the cheese and walnuts, mixing well. Fill each date with some of the cheese mixture. Wrap each stuffed date with the bacon until it goes all the way around the date. Secure with a toothpick.

Heat roughly 3 inches of the oil in a heavy-bottomed pot or a deep fryer until a candy thermometer registers 350°F. Carefully lower the dates into the hot oil, 10 at a time so as not to overcrowd the fryer. Fry until the dates are golden brown, about 4 minutes. Serve on a platter and drizzle the balsamic glaze over the dates.

Street Markets

Ponce City Market

The year 2014 just might be the most exciting year in Atlanta's urban history. It's the year the city completes the largest adaptive reuse project ever: the historic 1.1 million-square-foot Sears, Roebuck & Company building reopened as Ponce City Market (poncecitymarket.com), home to dozens of shops, office space, residential flats, and (most importantly, in my opinion) restaurants. Not only is this project an exciting addition to Atlanta's food scene, but it's also an instrumental component of the city's efforts to become more pedestrian friendly. It's huge, literally and figuratively. As I write this, the market, which is being developed by the same folks responsible for the trendy Westside Provisions District, is still under construction. But here's what we know: Anne Quatrano is opening a casual fish shack called Dub's Fish Camp near Linton Hopkins's (of Atlanta's Holeman & Finch and Restaurant Eugene) two new concepts: H&F Burger and H&F Bakery. The renowned Peter Chang of Tasty China will launch an authentic Szechuan spot—you can tame the fire afterward at chef-owner Wes Jones's Honeysuckle Gelato, his first brick-and-mortar location. There's also going to be a Korean street-food stall, Simply Seoul, turning out artisanal kimchee and steamed buns, making Ponce City Market a foodie's paradise.

Krog Street Market

Ponce City Market might be the largest space to open in Atlanta in 2014, but Inman Park's Krog Street Market is equally groundbreaking. Situated just off the BeltLine, the West Coast–inspired market is a food lover's dream. Housed in a converted 1920s single-story manufacturing warehouse, the 35,000-square-foot market plays host to a profusion of restaurants, including a Mex-Tex concept from Ford Fry, an American brasserie from *Top Chef* alum Eli Kirshtein (see The Luminary's profile on page 176) and a sandwich sanctuary (Fred's Meat & Bread) from The General Muir's Todd Ginsberg, who's also opening a Middle Eastern restaurant at the market called Yalla. The international options abound—I can't wait to check out Craft Izakaya, a mecca for Japanese small plates and sushi, Gu's Dumplings (see Gu's Bistro on page 114) and Asha Gomez's (of Cardamom Hill) Indian chicken stall called Spice Road Chicken. There are also more than two dozen market stalls, including a butchery and charcuterie shop (the Spotted Trotter), an international bakery with Hispanic and European leanings (Pannus Bakery), and a wine and beer shop from beloved Hop City. When can I move in?

Chai Pani

406 West Ponce de Leon Avenue
Decatur, GA 30030
(404) 378-4030
chaipanidecatur.com
Owners: Meherwan and Molly Irani
Chef de Cuisine: Daniel Peach

Most Indian restaurants in America feature northern Indian cuisine—in fact, the majority are so laser-focused that Meherwan Irani, a London-born, Indian-raised restaurateur who now calls America home, jokingly dubbed the cuisine banquet food ("We only eat things like tikka masala on very special occasions."). In reality, southern Indian food is as different from northern as German is from Italian, insists Irani, who opened Chai Pani with his wife, Molly, in Asheville, North Carolina, in an attempt to bring the rest of India to the table—the self-taught cook even brought in his mother to train his kitchen crew. Though expanding was never in the couple's plans, Decatur came calling. The James Beard nominee seamlessly transitioned the former Watershed space into a second, larger Chai Pani, representing the vibrancy of Indian street food and authentic home cooking. Expect bright flavors often soured by tamarind and sweetened with yogurt and an addictive combo of textures from explosive little bites called *chaat* (which means "to lick"—as in finger-licking good) and traditional *thalis* entrees. While Irani employs southern ingredients, the techniques are bona fide Indian—just look at his addictive okra fries: slivers of the southern staple are fried up until ultra crunchy and then doused with lime juice and salt. But perhaps most unexpected at the super-casual ethnic eatery is the quality of ingredients. Irani grows his own herbs, makes all chutneys, sauces, and spice blends in house and sources from many of the same local farms that top-tier restaurants use. No wonder there's almost always a line!

Corn Bhel

(SERVES 6)

6 medium ears of corn, husks on
2 cloves garlic
¼ cup rice vinegar
¼ cup fresh lime juice
¾ teaspoon salt
1 teaspoon sugar
¾ teaspoon freshly ground pepper
¼ cup finely chopped red onion or shallot
¼ cup chopped cilantro, stems removed
1½ teaspoon ground cumin
1½ cups light olive oil or canola oil (don't use extra-virgin)
1 cup diced, seeded cucumber
1 cup diced red onion
1 cup diced Roma tomatoes
½ cup fresh roughly chopped cilantro leaves, stems discarded
4 mint leaves, thinly sliced into strips
2 cups corn poha (can substitute pita chips, tortilla strips, or croutons)

Preheat the oven to 500°F. Roast the corn on a baking sheet until the husk can be peeled back to reveal lightly browned kernels, about 40 minutes. Let cool; shave kernels into a large serving bowl.

Meanwhile, add the next nine ingredients (garlic through cumin) to a food processor and puree on medium-low speed. Increase the speed to medium high and stream the olive oil in slowly until emulsified. Set the cumin-lime dressing aside.

To the bowl of corn, add the cucumbers, onions, tomatoes, cilantro, mint, and corn poha. Add the cumin-lime dressing to taste and toss like a salad.

Sloppy Jai (Kheema Paav)

(SERVES 8)

- ¼ cup canola oil
- 1 tablespoon cumin seeds
- 1 teaspoon roughly crushed black peppercorns (set grinder to coarse setting)
- 2 cups diced yellow onion, plus more for garnish
- 1 tablespoon kosher salt
- 1 tablespoon finely diced ginger (peel skin off with a spoon)
- 1 teaspoon green chiles (serranos preferred)
- 2 tablespoons ginger-garlic paste (see Note 1)
- 2 tablespoons ground coriander
- 1 tablespoon ground turmeric
- 2 tablespoons ground cumin
- 1 teaspoon red chili powder (don't use cayenne)
- ¼ cup roughly chopped cilantro
- 2 pounds ground lamb (coarse grind preferred)
- ½ cup plain yogurt (not Greek or flavored)
- 2 cups crushed vine-ripened tomatoes
- 1 tablespoon brown sugar
- 1 tablespoon apple cider vinegar (can substitute rice vinegar or white vinegar)
- 1 tablespoon garam masala (homemade preferred, see Note 2)
- 8 paav (can substitute any sweet, soft white roll), split and toasted with a touch of butter
- Sweetened yogurt, for garnish (mix equal parts sugar with plain yogurt, whisk until dissolved)

Heat a large wide sauté pan to medium-high. Add the oil and heat to near smoking. Add the cumin seeds and black peppercorns and allow seeds to sputter for a minute. Remove the pan from heat, add the diced yellow onion and salt, and return to medium-high heat. Sauté the onions until golden brown, about 15 to 20 minutes. Add the ginger and chiles and sauté until chiles are soft, about 3 minutes. Add the ginger-garlic paste and sauté until it starts to brown, about 3 to 5 minutes. Add the coriander, turmeric, cumin, red chili powder, and cilantro, and sauté for 1 minute.

Meanwhile, add the lamb to the sauté pan, increasing the heat to high. Sear the lamb for 5 minutes, ensuring all the meat is exposed to the cooking surface so it can properly brown. Add the yogurt and continue cooking until the lamb is glossy, about 10 minutes. Add the crushed tomatoes, sugar, vinegar, and garam masala. Simmer on medium heat for 15 minutes, adding salt to taste.

Spoon the lamb mixture on the toasted rolls and garnish with cilantro, diced onions, and a drizzle of sweetened yogurt.

Note 1: Add equal amounts peeled garlic and peeled ginger to a food processor with a few drops of oil. Blend to a smooth paste.

Note 2: To make garam masala, add 1 teaspoon whole black peppercorns, 1 teaspoon cumin seeds, 2 small sticks cinnamon, 4 cloves, 1 dried bay leaf, and 4 whole green cardamom pods into a dry pan. Toast on low heat until you can smell the spices, about 2 minutes. Cool the spices and grind in a coffee grinder. Store in solid airtight container.

Malabar Chicken Curry

(SERVES 4)

½ cup plus 1 tablespoon vegetable oil, divided
1½ teaspoons mustard seeds
½ teaspoon fenugreek seeds
12 to 15 curry leaves, finely chopped
2 to 3 small dried red chiles
2½ tablespoons grated ginger
4 cups chopped red onions
1 teaspoon chili powder
1½ tablespoons ground coriander
1 teaspoon ground turmeric
½ cup chopped cilantro (leaves and stems)
3 cups chopped tomatoes
1 teaspoon salt
2 tablespoons fresh lime juice
1 cup unsweetened coconut milk
2 pounds boneless, skinless chicken breast, cut into bite-size pieces
2 cups basmati rice, cooked to package instructions

Pour ½ cup oil into a large saucepan over medium heat. Once the oil is hot, add the mustard seeds, fenugreek seeds, curry leaves, and red chiles and sauté for 2 minutes. Add the ginger and onions, reduce heat to medium-low, and allow the onions to brown and soften, about 30 minutes. Add the chili powder, coriander, turmeric, and cilantro and mix together. Increase the heat to medium and add the tomatoes, salt, and lime juice. Simmer, stirring occasionally, until the tomatoes have disintegrated and the oil separates out, about 15 to 20 minutes. Add ½ cup water and the coconut milk. Bring to a boil, then reduce heat to medium-low.

Meanwhile, in a large skillet, heat the remaining 1 tablespoon oil over high heat. Add the chicken to the skillet and brown on all sides, leaving the centers pink, about 2 to 4 minutes.

Add the chicken to the curry and simmer until the chicken has cooked through, about 5 to 7 minutes. Serve over basmati rice.

Concentrics Restaurants

concentricsrestaurants.com
Owner/Founder: Robert Amick

ONE. midtown kitchen

559 Dutch Valley Road NE
Atlanta, GA 30324
(404) 892-4111
onemidtownkitchen.com
Executive Chef: Nick Oltarsh

The Brasserie and Neighborhood Cafe at Parish

240 North Highland Avenue NE
Atlanta, GA 30307
(404) 681-4434
parishatl.com
Executive Chef: Zeb Stevenson

TAP

1180 Peachtree Street NE
Atlanta, GA 30309
(404) 347-2220
tapat1180.com
Executive Chef: Nick McCormick

The Spence

75 5th Street NW
Atlanta, GA 30308
(404) 892-9111
thespenceatl.com
Owner and Executive Chef: Richard Blais
Executive Chef: Adrian Villarreal

TWO urban licks

820 Ralph McGill Boulevard NE
Atlanta, GA 30306
(404) 522-4622
twourbanlicks.com
Executive Chef: Todd Stein

Bob Amick may have built his career in corporate restaurants like Peasant Restaurants, Morton's, and Killer Creek, but today he runs five of the most unique, chef-driven concepts in town. "I took some time off and realized I wanted to do something more off the beaten path, something clearly accessible, not too pricy and geared toward locals rather than business," says Amick. In 2002, ONE. midtown kitchen was born, one of the city's first high-profile restaurants to open in a seedy location, serve small plates, and offer every wine on the list by the bottle, glass, half glass, and even a bottomless option (they were also the first to do keg wines). "We were instrumental in revitalizing Midtown, showing others you didn't have to do main on Main," says the James Beard nominee, who brought in his son, daughter, and daughter-in-law to work with him. "Success breeds more success, so we decided to do more restaurants."

Next came TWO urban licks, "which was always just meant to be fun." It's a big warehouse with skyline views, live music, and food meant to make you lick your fingers (like their signature smoked salmon chips—they've sold over 300,000 since opening). A 9 foot, wood-pit rotisserie anchors the dining room, while an outdoor bocce ball court overlooks the Beltline. It's no wonder TWO does 1,000 covers on a Friday night, despite its notoriously suspicious location.

Next came TAP, a neighborhood gastropub, and PARISH, a 2-story breakfast-lunch-dinner eatery with an American brasserie upstairs and a market-cafe down below. And in 2012, Amick, along with *Top Chef All-Stars* winner Richard Blais, opened the group's boldest restaurant: The Spence. "We call it a big city neighborhood restaurant—it's a pretty small spot with a seasonally driven menu of interesting small plates that change all the time. It's our hippest restaurant and most adventuresome menu." Agreed. I love bringing friends to The Spence, cluttering our table up with small plates like the Thai-style brussels sprouts (which sub in cauliflower when it comes into season) and bone marrow piled with tuna tartare.

Despite being a restaurant group, each of Amick's restaurants feel uniquely independent. "Concentrics is not a legal entity, it's just a brand because we had to refer to ourselves as something. But all of our restaurants have different personalities driven by their chefs," explains Amick, who also offers design, development, and management services to aspiring restaurants. "We are first and foremost restaurant guys—just like artists with a blank canvas, creating something new every time."

The Spence's Baby Kale Caesar

(SERVES 4)

4 egg yolks
1 tablespoon anchovy paste
2 tablespoons Dijon mustard
1 tablespoon freshly ground black pepper, plus more to taste
12 garlic cloves
3 tablespoons capers
1 teaspoon salt, plus more to taste
Zest of 2 lemons
6 tablespoons lemon juice
6 tablespoons red wine vinegar
⅓ cup freshly grated Parmesan cheese, plus ½ cup for garnish
4 cups grapeseed oil
1 tablespoon garlic chili oil
Salt and pepper to taste
8 cups mixed baby kale
4 tablespoons croutons (homemade preferred)
4 teaspoons tarragon leaves
1 lemon

In a blender puree the first seven ingredients (egg yolks though 1 teaspoon salt). Add the lemon zest and juice, red wine vinegar, and ⅓ cup Parmesan and puree again. With the blender at half speed, stream in the oils until the dressing is emulsified. Adjust with a little bit of cold water. Adjust seasoning as needed.

In a large bowl, mix the kale, croutons, and tarragon together. Season with salt and pepper to taste. Squeeze the lemon on top and toss to coat, garnish with the remaining ½ cup grated Parmesan, and serve.

The Spence's Crispy Thai Brussels Sprouts

(SERVES 4–6)

Kosher salt
1 pound brussels sprouts, core removed, halved lengthwise
3 cloves garlic, peeled
1 Thai chile pepper
½ cup sugar
½ cup fish sauce
½ cup lime juice
½ cup water
1 sprig mint, leaves torn
3 sprigs cilantro, leaves torn
¼ red onion, thinly sliced
¼ cup peanut oil

Fill a medium pot with water and season with a handful of kosher salt. Bring to a boil over high heat. Once boiling, add the brussels sprouts and cook until just undercooked, about 2 to 3 minutes. Remove the sprouts and place in an ice-water bath to stop the cooking process. Remove the sprouts from water and pat with a paper towel to dry well.

In a blender combine the garlic, Thai chile, sugar, fish sauce, lime juice, and water to make a vinaigrette. Puree until smooth and only small flecks of the chile remain.

In a large mixing bowl, combine the mint, cilantro, and onion. Pour vinaigrette over top and toss to combine.

In a medium pot over medium heat, add the peanut oil to cover the bottom by ½ inch. Add the blanched brussels sprouts in a single layer and sear until golden and crispy, flipping if necessary, about 2 minutes. Add the crispy sprouts to the bowl of herbs and toss in the sauce until the sprouts are dressed. Serve.

THE SPENCE'S JUICY LUCY

(SERVES 6)

1 pound chuck
1 pound brisket
½ pound short ribs
½ pound dry-aged beef fat
12 slices white American cheese, quartered
6 (3-inch) brioche burger buns
1 cup caramelized Vidalia onions
½ cup pickles

Chill a meat grinder, the meat, and the beef fat in the freezer until meat starts to stiffen, about 30 minutes. Grind the chuck, brisket, short ribs, and beef fat through the grinder. Mix all of the ground meats together and form into 12 4-ounce patties with your hands.

Center 8 quarters of cheese between 2 patties. Be sure to seal the burger meat well, using your hands to form an 8-ounce patty encapsulating the cheese. (*Note:* Ensure there is no visible cheese or seams.)

Place patties on a grill preheated to medium. Cook for 5 to 7 minutes per side. Place the cooked patties on the buns and garnish with the caramelized onions and pickles.

TWO URBAN LICKS' SMOKED GOUDA GRITS

(SERVES 4)

2 cups whole milk
2 cups water
1½ teaspoons kosher salt
1 cup coarse ground grits
½ teaspoon freshly ground black pepper
4 tablespoons (½ stick) unsalted butter
4 ounces smoked Gouda cheese, shredded

Place the milk, water, and salt into a large, heavy-bottomed pot over medium-high heat and bring to a boil. Once the milk mixture comes to a boil, gradually add the grits while continually whisking. Once all of the grits have been incorporated, decrease the heat to low and cover. Cook until the grits are creamy, about 20 to 25 minutes, removing the lid and whisking every 3 to 4 minutes to prevent lumps. Remove the grits from heat, add the pepper and butter, and whisk to combine. Once the butter is melted, gradually whisk in the cheese, a little at a time. Serve immediately once the cheese is melted.

TWO urban licks' Smoked Salmon Chips with Chipotle Cream Cheese

(SERVES 6–8)

½ pound cream cheese, room temperature
1 (3-ounce) can chipotles in adobo sauce
¼ cup finely snipped chives, plus more for garnish
Juice of 1 lime
½ tablespoon kosher salt
½ tablespoon sugar
6 cups canola oil for frying
2 Idaho potatoes, thinly sliced on a mandoline to $\frac{1}{16}$ inch
2 tablespoons barbecue seasoning (McCormick's preferred)
½ pound smoked salmon
1 small red onion, diced
1 (2-ounce) jar capers, drained

Place the cream cheese in a mixing bowl and stir until softened and smooth. Add the chipotle chiles and puree with mixer until smooth. Add the chives, lime juice, salt, and sugar; mix well. Set aside.

Heat the oil in a heavy-bottomed pot or deep fryer until a candy thermometer reads 350°F. Carefully place potato slices into the hot oil and fry on both sides until golden brown, about 2 to 3 minutes. Remove chips from oil and drain on a plate lined with paper towels. Sprinkle with the barbecue seasoning.

To assemble, evenly spread the chipotle cream cheese across the potato chips with a butter knife. Place the smoked salmon on top (roughly ½ tablespoon per chip). Garnish with the red onions, capers, and chives. Serve.

Fifth Group Restaurants

fifthgroup.com

Partners: Robby Kukler, Steve Simon, and Kris Reinhard

Alma Cocina

191 Peachtree Street NE
Atlanta, GA 30303
(404) 968-9662
alma-atlanta.com

Executive Chef: Chad Clevenger

Ecco

40 7th Street NE
Atlanta, GA 30306
(404) 347-9555
ecco-atlanta.com

Executive Chef: Jonathan Beatty

El Taco

1186 North Highland Avenue NE
Atlanta, GA 30306
(404) 873-4656
eltaco-atlanta.com

Executive Chef: Scott Keefer

La Tavola

992 Virginia Avenue NE
Atlanta, GA 30306
(404) 873-5430
latavolatrattoria.com
Executive Chef: Brent Banda

Lure

1106 Crescent Avenue NE
Atlanta, GA 30306
(404) 817-3650
lure-atlanta.com
Executive Chef: David Bradley

South City Kitchen

1144 Crescent Avenue NE
Atlanta, GA 30309
(404) 873-7358
1675 Cumberland Parkway SE #401
Smyrna, GA 30080
(770) 435-0700
Executive Chef: Chip Ulbrich

Back in the early '90s, three twentysomethings set out to create a new kind of restaurant in Atlanta. They opened South City Kitchen, the city's first New Southern restaurant, merging regional ingredients and traditional recipes with contemporary style. "We always had the mind-set to grow a group overtime, one that opened fresh and innovative, yet classic and timeless, restaurants in neighborhoods," says Robby Kukler, one of Fifth Group's founders. "Restaurants that draw on all five senses and are based on the five groups of people we serve (hence the name): employees, guests, community, purveyors, and investors."

Kukler and his partners have since opened half a dozen one-of-a-kind restaurants under their umbrella, which is a bit of an oxymoron to me. When you have such a successful restaurant group, especially one that's not chef owned, there's a corporate connotation that exists—I have to admit, I expected generic food you could find in any chain. But Fifth Group is the opposite. Each of their restaurants is chef driven with seasonal menus sourcing from more than 20 farmers.

Perhaps most impressive is their sustainability. At La Tavola, an intimate trattoria serving clean Italian food, a patio garden provides herbs and vegetables for the

restaurant. Ecco, a European-inspired eatery, was the first restaurant in the state to eliminate dumpsters—they recycle or compost everything. In fact, 95 percent of the products that come through the group's doors are recycled or composted, annually diverting more than 500,000 pounds of waste destined for landfills. At the group's modern fish house, Lure, rainwater is harvested from the roof into a 3,000-gallon reclamation pillow used in the restrooms and to irrigate plantings and trees.

That makes me feel really great about digging into a plate of octopus lettuce wraps with Vietnamese sauce or the house-made smoked fish board (think charcuterie with trout pâté instead of chicken, and kingfish pastrami standing in for brisket). Not exactly chain food. Likewise, their modern Mexican spot Alma Cocina puts an upscale spin on Latin-inspired dishes, like Peruvian seviche and pork tamales, while the high-energy, family-friendly El Taco is a fresh Tex-Mex neighborhood joint complete with a spirited salsa bar, Mexican pizza, and dangerously delicious margaritas. I'll cheers to that.

Alma Cocina's Mexican White Shrimp Huarache

(SERVES 10)

1 pound Roma tomatoes, cut into bite-size pieces
3 avocados, halved
2 cups orange juice
2 pounds masa harina (corn flour)
4 tablespoons olive oil
4 tablespoons adobo sauce
6 tablespoons queso cotija (can substitute crumbled feta or Parmesan)
8 ounces (2 sticks) butter, divided
2½ pounds Mexican white shrimp, peeled, deveined, tails removed, and cut into 4 pieces
½ cup Sriracha sauce
Salt to taste
½ cup green onions, julienned

Cold smoke the Roma tomatoes with pecan wood for 3 minutes. (*Note:* You can grill the tomatoes if cold smoking isn't an option.)

Char the avocados (with skins) with a blowtorch until black, about 30 seconds. (*Note:* You can grill the avocados with a bit of oil if blowtorching isn't an option.)

In a medium saucepan over medium-high heat, reduce 2 cups orange juice to 1 cup, about 15 minutes. Set aside to cool.

Place the corn flour, olive oil, adobo sauce, and queso cotija together in a mixer fitted with a paddle attachment. Spin on medium speed until combined, about 3 minutes. Take ½ cup dough and roll it in the palm of your hand to make a football shape. Flatten the dough in a tortilla press or with a sauté pan lined with greased plastic wrap, pressing the dough into a sandal shape about ¼-inch thick. Remove the dough from the press or plastic wrap and place it on a sheet tray lined with parchment paper so it doesn't stick together. Cook each piece of dough on a dry skillet over medium heat and toast each side for 3 minutes. Set aside.

In a sauté pan over medium-high heat, add half of the butter. Once the butter starts to foam, add the shrimp and cook halfway, about 3 minutes. Deglaze the pan with the cup of reduced orange juice and Sriracha. Cook for 3 minutes. Add the smoked tomatoes and season with salt to taste. Remove the pan from heat and swirl in the remaining butter.

Add the shrimp to the huarache. Top with avocado and garnish with green onions. Serve immediately.

Ecco's Fried Goat Cheese with Honey & Black Pepper

(SERVES 6–8)

2 cups all-purpose flour
1 teaspoon baking soda
1 teaspoon salt
2 tablespoons honey
2¼ cups cold soda water
4 quarts oil for frying (canola preferred)
3 ounces fresh goat cheese, the dryer the better (Laura Chenel's goat cheese from California preferred)
4 cups flour for dredging, seasoned with salt and pepper
2 tablespoons honey, heated to very warm
¼ teaspoon freshly cracked black pepper

To make the batter, sift the flour and baking soda into a large mixing bowl. Stir in the salt. Add 2 tablespoons honey and whisk in the soda water until the batter is smooth. Refrigerate for 30 to 60 minutes.

In a heavy-bottomed pot or deep fryer, heat the oil to 350°F. Roll the goat cheese into ½-ounce balls. Chill until very cold, about 30 minutes. Roll the cold cheese balls in the seasoned flour. Working one or two at a time, roll the goat cheese in the batter and carefully drop into hot oil until lightly golden brown, about 1 to 2 minutes. (*Note:* Move the balls around to ensure they don't stick together.) Drain fried cheese on a cooling rack fitted in a sheet tray for 30 seconds.

Place the fried cheese balls in a warm bowl and garnish with the warm honey and cracked black pepper. Serve immediately.

El Taco's Coconut Flan

(SERVES 6)

1 cup sugar
¼ cup water
1 egg yolk
2 eggs
½ cup heavy cream
1 (27-ounce) can coconut milk
1 (28-ounce) can condensed milk (La Lechera or Eagle preferred)
1 tablespoon spiced rum

Add the sugar to a dry 6-inch saucepan. Carefully add the water and gently move sugar enough to just allow the water to completely moisten the sugar. Place the saucepan over medium-high heat. Without stirring, allow the sugar water to bubble and simmer until caramel color develops. Stir gently and cook until the sugar is the color of honey, 5 to 10 minutes depending on your stove. Carefully ladle 2 tablespoons of the caramel into 6-ounce ceramic or glass ramekins. Allow to cool.

Preheat oven to 325°F. In a large mixing bowl whisk the egg yolk, eggs, and heavy cream together until smooth. Add the coconut milk and whisk until incorporated. Add the condensed milk and rum, whisking until smooth and creamy. Ladle 4 ounces into each of the caramel-lined ramekins.

Place the ramekins into a deep casserole dish. Cover the entire dish with foil, leaving one corner uncovered. Place the dish on a rack in the middle of the oven. Carefully add enough water to the baking dish to create a water bath surrounding the ramekins. (*Note:* The water level should reach the same depth as the liquid inside the ramekins.) Carefully finish covering the final corner with foil, taking care not to allow any water to splash into the ramekins.

Bake for 75 minutes, until the flan is slightly firm and jiggly, like Jell-O. Remove the dish from the oven and allow to cool to room temperature in the water bath, about 1 hour.

Remove the ramekins from water and transfer to the refrigerator for at least 3 hours, until the custard is completely set. (*Note:* Chilling overnight is preferred.)

To serve, carefully run a knife around the edge of the ramekins to loosen the flan. Invert the ramekins onto a serving plate and gently shake until the flan releases. (*Note:* The caramel will release liquid, which becomes the sauce that is drizzled over the flan for serving.)

Optional: Drizzle with a fruit sauce or puree, like mango or passion fruit.

La Tavola's Braised Duck & Ricotta Gnocchi

(SERVES 4–6)

For the gnocchi:

1 pound fresh ricotta, chilled
1 large egg
1 tablespoon olive oil
½ teaspoon salt, plus more for cooking
⅛ teaspoon grated nutmeg
½ cup unbleached all-purpose flour, plus more as needed
Freshly grated Parmigiano Reggiano and olive oil for serving

For the duck:

4 sprigs rosemary
4 sprigs thyme
2 ounces dry porcini mushrooms
2 pounds chopped onions
2 pounds chopped carrots
1 quart white wine
8 ounces canned San Marzano tomatoes
8 duck legs, cleaned of excess fat
Salt and pepper
1 quart chicken stock, warmed

To make the gnocchi: Wrap the ricotta in a cheesecloth and tie butcher's twine around the wrapped cheese. Hang the wrapped cheese in the refrigerator with a bowl placed underneath to catch the liquid and let rest overnight.

In a medium stainless bowl, mix the drained ricotta, egg, olive oil, salt, and nutmeg. Slowly add the flour to incorporate, adding more flour as needed until the dough is slightly sticky and rounded. Place a kitchen towel over the dough and let sit at room temperature for 20 minutes.

When ready to roll the gnocchi, flour a wooden table or cutting board. Take ¼ of the dough and gently roll it out into a log. Cut the log into ½-inch pieces.

Meanwhile, bring salted water to a medium boil in a large pot. Once boiling, drop the gnocchi into the water and cook until they rise to the surface, about 2 minutes. Drain well.

To make the duck: Make a bouquet garni with the rosemary and thyme.

Hydrate the porcini mushrooms in 1 quart water per package instructions.

In a large skillet over medium heat, add the onions, carrots, bouquet garni, and hydrated porcini mushrooms. Sauté until the onions are caramelized, about 8 to 10 minutes. Add the wine and tomatoes; cook over medium-low heat for 1 hour.

Preheat the oven to 300°F. Season the duck legs with salt and pepper. Place the duck legs in a large braising pot over medium heat and sear until golden brown, about 10 minutes. Turn the legs over and cook for another 4 minutes.

Cover the duck legs with the tomato-mushroom mixture and chicken stock. Place into oven for 2½ hours. Remove from the oven and allow to cool. Strain the liquid; set aside.

Once the legs are cool, use your hands to pull the meat away from the bone, discarding any fat.

Add the duck meat to the strained liquid and cook in a 6-quart stockpot for 40 minutes.

To plate: Add the cooked gnocchi to the duck sauce and cook over medium heat until the sauce starts to stick to the gnocchi, about 2 minutes. Turn the heat off and plate in a large serving bowl. Grate fresh Parmigiano Reggiano on top and drizzle your favorite Italian olive oil over the dish. Serve.

Lure's Crab Dip

(SERVES 4)

- 6 ounces peekytoe crabmeat, picked through for shells
- 2 tablespoons mayonnaise
- 1½ ounce hot sauce (Crystal preferred)
- ¾ teaspoon Old Bay Seasoning
- ¾ teaspoon white vinegar
- 1 large tomato, cut into ¼-inch slices
- 1 sprig thyme, leaves removed
- 2 teaspoons extra-virgin olive oil
- Salt and pepper to taste
- 1 tablespoons crème fraîche
- 2 tablespoons minced chives
- 1 baguette, cut into ¼-inch slices and toasted

Preheat oven to 350°F. In a large bowl, combine the crabmeat, mayonnaise, hot sauce, Old Bay, and vinegar. Fold together and refrigerate.

Meanwhile, place the tomato slices on a parchment-lined cookie sheet. Sprinkle with the thyme leaves, drizzle with the olive oil, and season with salt and pepper. Roast until softened, about 20 to 25 minutes. Remove from the oven and allow to cool. Once cooled, remove the skins from the tomato and tear into large pieces.

Raise oven temperature to 400°F. Place the roasted tomatoes in a small oven-safe dish. Top with the crab mixture, and spoon the crème fraîche into the center of the crab; sprinkle with the chives. Bake until the dip bubbles, about 5 to 10 minutes. Serve with toasted baguette slices.

South City Kitchen's She-Crab Soup

(SERVES 6–8)

½ pound (2 sticks) unsalted butter
1 medium yellow onion, diced
1 rib celery, sliced
1 tablespoon chopped garlic
2 bay leaves
1 teaspoon chopped fresh thyme
½ teaspoon nutmeg
3 tablespoons Old Bay Seasoning
1 cup all-purpose flour
½ gallon whole milk, plus more as needed
2 cups heavy cream
2 tablespoons hot sauce
2 tablespoons Worcestershire sauce
2 cups crab stock (can substitute clam juice), plus more as needed
Salt and fresh black pepper to taste
1 pound blue-crab claw meat, picked clean of shell
1 cup dry sherry

Melt the butter in a heavy-bottomed stockpot over medium heat. Add the onion, celery, and garlic and sauté until softened, about 5 minutes. Add the bay leaves, thyme, nutmeg, and Old Bay, and let sweat for a few more minutes

Stir in the flour and whisk until smooth to create a roux. Cook for 5 minutes over low heat, stirring frequently. Add the milk, cream, hot sauce, Worcestershire, and crab stock, whisking thoroughly to remove all lumps. Bring to a simmer, stirring frequently to keep from scorching, and cook for 10 minutes. Add more milk or stock if needed to adjust consistency.

Strain soup through a fine sieve and return to heat. Season to taste with salt and pepper. Gently stir in the crab and sherry. Adjust seasoning to taste. Serve immediately.

Public Markets

One of the best parts about living in the South is the amazing bounty of locally grown produce we're privy to. From juicy Georgia peaches to heirloom tomatoes, pastured chicken to grass-fed beef, the opportunity for fresh, farm-grown food is seemingly endless. So it's no surprise the city plays host to an abundance of farmers' markets. To wit, a guide to five of the city's best:

Piedmont Park Green Market: Set in a 25-acre 1904 Frederick Law Olmstead-designed park in the heart of the city, this market is a mix of farmers and added-value products like artisan bread, small-batch peanut butter, and handmade soap. Started in 2003, the market (open Saturday from March to December) hosts some 40-odd vendors during peak season, alongside live music, local artists, and chef demos. If you want to fit in, bring your pooch.

Buford Highway Farmers' Market: If you're on the hunt for that oddball Asian spice (did someone say galangal?), head to this colossal market, a mecca for dirt-cheap ethnic ingredients from around the globe. Whether you need *gochujang* for Korean bibimbap or cassava for Brazilian tapioca, you can find it at this international institution, which is also home to one of the largest fresh produce departments, whole-fish seafood counters, and meat cases in the city. As expected, the unexpected abounds, from oxtails and tripe to live lobsters and half a dozen varieties of eggplant.

Morningside Farmers' Market: Since 1995, this farmers' cooperative-turned-market has been selling locally grown produce to hungry Atlantans every Saturday morning. It's the perfect spot for people who want to put a face to their fiddleheads, and one of the few year-round markets in town, not to mention the only market that requires all produce to be certified organic. Don't miss the chef demos and irresistible pies.

DeKalb Farmers' Market: To call this megastore a farmers' market is a bit deceiving—there are no farmers personally handing you fresh tomatoes here. But it's a cornerstone in Atlanta's market scene in its own right, serving over 100,000 people each week. Not only will you be hard-pressed to beat the prices here, but the 140,000-square-foot market sources primarily organically grown and non-GMO produce from around the world and was one of the city's founding fathers in the fresh fish department—you'll find more than 450 varieties, many whole or live, all of which can be cut or filleted to order. Equally impressive is the vast collection of international and exotic products.

Peachtree Road Farmers Market: The brainchild of Gina and Linton Hopkins of Restaurant Eugene and the Cathedral of St. Philip, this farmers' market is the largest producer-only (i.e., every single product has been grown, raised, or made by the seller) farmers' market in the state. Like clockwork, every Saturday morning from April through December, the market opens to the public, offering exclusively Georgia-grown products, most of which are certified organic. Its humble beginnings with 12 vendors in the church parking lot are long gone; today you'll find more than 70 vendors alongside near-weekly demonstrations from chefs who have been nominated by the farmers. BYOBag—it's greener—and pay with cash.

Ford Fry

Owner and Executive Chef: Ford Fry

JCT. Kitchen & Bar

1198 Howell Mill Road #18
Atlanta, GA 30318
(404) 355-2252
jctkitchen.com
Executive Chef: E. J. Hodgkinson

King + Duke

3060 Peachtree Road NW
Atlanta, GA 30305
(404) 477-3500
kinganddukeatl.com
Executive Chef: Joe Schafer

No. 246

129 East Ponce de Leon Avenue
Decatur, GA 30030
(678) 399-8246
no246.com
Chef de Cuisine: Andrew Isabella

St. Cecilia

3455 Peachtree Road NE
Atlanta, GA 30326
(404) 554-9995
stceciliaatl.com
Chef de Cuisine: Craig Richards

The Optimist

914 Howell Mill Road
Atlanta, GA 30318
(404) 477-6260
theoptimistrestaurant.com
Executive Chef: Adam Evans

If you're coming to Atlanta for the first time, odds are someone's going to take you to JCT. Kitchen & Bar, a Southern-inspired, bi-level restaurant serving traditional favorites (did somebody say fried chicken?) against a backdrop of the Atlanta skyline. It's a restaurant that epitomizes the city of Atlanta arguably more than any other restaurant in town. It's also owned by Ford Fry, a Texas native, New England Culinary Institute alum, guitar-playing James Beard nominee who operates five of Atlanta's hottest restaurants. Though Fry manned the stove at JCT. every day for five years, today (nearly a decade later) he's the front man for his restaurants, each of which has an insanely talented chef running the kitchen.

"We have five restaurants, but I'm fighting really hard to not be looked at as a group," says Fry. "I hate taking the credit—it's all about the chef on-site, that's who I'm trying to promote." As such, each of Fry's restaurants are vastly different from one another, energized by distinctive regions or techniques, and thus admittedly "not everything to everybody."

While JCT. Kitchen is inspired by the South, No. 246 in Decatur draws inspiration from California-style Italian cuisine. On the Westside, The Optimist (named one of *Esquire*'s Best New Restaurants in 2012) revolves around American coastlines—expect a bounty of fresh oysters and sustainable seafood. And up in Buckhead, King + Duke is anchored by wood-hearth cooking. "It's about going against modernist cuisine, back to a time when cooks worked over fire pits and burning wood," says Fry, noting that even vegetables get the inferno treatment as they're roasted directly on the coals. For as masculine and warm as King + Duke is, up the street St. Cecilia is commensurately feminine and airy, exerting bright, citrusy flavors and simple preparations of grilled fish and raw crudos.

For as varied as Fry's restaurants might be, there are some common denominators: They're all laid-back and welcoming; they all begin with regionally sourced ingredients; and they're all good, plain and simple. "There's a lot of food coming out today that's more interesting than delicious, but I lean more toward just solid food—at the end of the day, it just needs to taste good." No wonder JCT. sells more than half a million "Angry" Mussel bowls every year—it just tastes so darn good.

JCT.'s "Angry" Mussels with Vidalia Onion, Bacon & Chile

(SERVES 1–2)

3 ounces diced smoked bacon
1 clove garlic, sliced
¼ Vidalia onion, sliced thin
1 serrano chile, sliced
1 pound mussels (Prince Edward Island preferred), cleaned
¼ cup dry white wine
½ cup (1 stick) cold unsalted butter
1 teaspoon kosher salt
2 tablespoons minced chives
Rustic toast for dipping

Render the bacon in a large skillet over medium-high heat until it begins to crisp, about 4 minutes. Once the bacon is almost crisp, increase the heat to high and add the garlic, onion, and serrano chile. Cook for 1 to 2 minutes and then add the mussels. Stir until the mussels start to open. Deglaze the pan with the wine and cook until evaporated, about 3 minutes. Add the cold butter and keep stirring until the butter is almost completely melted, about 3 to 4 minutes. Remove the skillet from heat and season with kosher salt. Garnish with fresh cut chives and serve with thick rustic toast for sopping the broth.

King + Duke's Smoked Half Chicken with Sweet Onions & Salad

(SERVES 4)

2 quarts water
1 cup salt
½ cup sugar
1 lemon, sliced
2 sprigs thyme
1 tablespoon black peppercorns
2 bay leaves
1 (3- to 4-pound) organic chicken, split in half, backbone removed
2 sweet onions, peeled and sliced ½-inch thick
2 tablespoons plus ¼ cup extra-virgin olive oil, divided
Salt and pepper to taste
12 ounces mixed lettuces and chicories (organic preferred)
Juice of 5 lemons
2 tablespoons chopped fresh herbs (parsley, sage, rosemary, thyme suggested)

At least one day before serving, combine the first seven ingredients (water through bay leaves) in a large sauce pot over high heat. Cook until the sugar and salt have dissolved, about 5 minutes. Remove from heat and cool to room temperature. Place the chicken in the brine and refrigerate overnight.

Remove the chicken from the brine and pat dry. Place the chicken on a sheet pan fitted with a cooling rack and refrigerate, uncovered, for at least 3 hours (overnight is preferred).

Preheat a grill to 250°F. Meanwhile, toss the sliced onions in 2 tablespoons olive oil, salt, and pepper. Place the chicken and marinated onions on the grill over indirect heat, skin side up. Smoke the chicken and onions until the internal temperature of the chicken registers 160°F at the thigh/leg joint, about 45 to 60 minutes. Allow to rest for 10 minutes.

Meanwhile, toss the lettuces and chicories in the lemon juice, the remaining ¼ cup olive oil, and herbs. Season with salt and pepper. Serve alongside smoked chicken and onions.

No. 246's Bistecca

(SERVES 4)

¼ cup toasted almonds
2¼ cup piquillo peppers
½ cup roasted tomatoes
2 garlic cloves, peeled
3 tablespoons red wine vinegar
1 tablespoon smoked paprika
¼ cup day-old or toasted bread, crust removed
⅓ cup plus ⅛ cup extra-virgin olive oil, divided
Kosher salt and fresh cracked black pepper to taste
1 (40-ounce) bone-in rib eye
½ cup (1 stick) unsalted butter, melted
4 to 6 sprigs fresh rosemary

In a food processor, finely grind the almonds. Add the peppers, tomatoes, garlic, vinegar, and paprika; puree well, scraping down the sides with a rubber spatula. Add the bread and process well. Transfer to a mixing bowl and fold in ⅓ cup olive oil gently with a rubber spatula. Season to taste with salt and pepper. Set the romesco sauce aside.

Preheat a grill to 500°F. Brush the rib eye with ⅛ cup olive oil and season heavily with salt and pepper. Grill the steak uncovered for 6 to 7 minutes, flip and baste the charred side with melted butter. Cover and cook for another 8 minutes for medium-rare, basting occasionally. Once the steak is almost done, lay the rosemary over the steak and baste one more time with the remaining butter to allow the rosemary flavor to coat the meat. Take the steak off and allow it to rest on a drain rack for 7 minutes. Slice the steak and serve with the romesco sauce.

St. Cecilia's Spaghetti with Crab & Chiles

(SERVES 4)

Salt
1 pound dried spaghetti
2 tablespoons canola oil
5 cloves garlic, sliced thin
1 serrano chile, sliced thin
Pinch of chile flakes
½ cup white wine
1 tablespoon unsalted butter
½ pound fresh crab (jumbo lump preferred)
Juice and zest of 1 lemon
Torn Italian parsley leaves for garnish
Torn mint for garnish
Extra-virgin olive oil for garnish

Bring a large pot of salted water to a boil. Cook spaghetti 2 minutes less than package instructions, gently stirring occasionally. Drain and set aside.

Meanwhile, heat the canola oil in a sauté pan over medium-high heat. Add the garlic, serrano, and chile flakes. Cook until garlic is slightly golden, about 10 seconds. Remove the pan from heat and add the wine. Return the pan to heat and continue cooking until the wine is reduced by half, about 30 seconds. Add the cooked pasta and toss gently to coat with the sauce. Add the butter, crab, and lemon juice and continue stirring until butter melts. Serve in a large, warm bowl or four separate bowls and garnish with the lemon zest, torn parsley and mint, and a drizzle of olive oil.

The Optimist's Duck & Andouille Sausage Gumbo

(SERVES 4–6)

1 whole duck, cut into 8 pieces, bones reserved
Kosher salt and cayenne pepper to taste
8 ounces diced andouille sausage
⅓ cup canola oil
¾ cup all-purpose flour
3½ tablespoons unsalted butter
1 large poblano pepper, finely diced
1 large yellow onion, finely diced
1½ cups finely diced celery
3 cloves garlic, sliced
2 quarts chicken broth (homemade preferred)
2 bay leaves
⅛ cup smoked paprika
1 teaspoon freshly ground black pepper
½ teaspoon cayenne pepper
⅛ cup Worcestershire sauce
2½ tablespoons hot sauce (Tabasco Sauce or Crystal preferred)

Season the duck generously with the kosher salt and lightly with the cayenne pepper. Place a large cast-iron skillet over medium-high heat. Add the duck and reserved bones and brown for 10 minutes. Set aside.

To the same skillet, add the andouille and brown for 10 minutes. Set aside, keeping the rendered fat in the skillet.

Reduce heat to medium and add the oil and flour to the skillet, whisking until smooth to make a roux. Cook until the roux is slightly lighter than dark chocolate, about 45 minutes. Remove the roux from the skillet and set aside.

In a soup pot over medium-high heat, melt the butter. Add the pepper, onion, celery, and garlic, and continue to cook until soft, about 15 minutes.

Add the chicken broth and bring to a boil. Reduce heat to a simmer and whisk in the roux, duck, sausage, and the remaining ingredients. Once the duck pieces are fully cooked, remove them and allow to cool slightly. Shred the meat and set it aside. Let the gumbo simmer for 1 hour; season with kosher salt. Add the shredded duck back into the gumbo. Remove the pot from heat, let come to room temperature, and chill in the refrigerator overnight.

When ready to eat, scrape off the solid fat that has risen to the top and slowly heat the gumbo over medium-low heat. Serve.

Optional: Serve with steamed rice and garlic bread.

Fox Bros. Bar-B-Q

1238 DeKalb Avenue NE
Atlanta, GA 30307
(404) 577-4030
foxbrosbbq.com

Owners and Executive Chefs: Jonathan and Justin Fox

Some chefs go to cooking school. Some apprentice under Michelin-starred chefs. Jonathan and Justin Fox, twin brothers from San Antonio, Texas, are self-taught—they also got their start cooking at Six Flags. Not exactly what you'd expect from two chefs who run one of Atlanta's most beloved restaurants. But Fox Bros. Bar-B-Q isn't your average Atlanta restaurant. For starters, the city isn't exactly known for great 'cue. Scratch that—before the brothers Fox opened their restaurant in 2007, the city *wasn't* exactly known for great 'cue. But these two put Atlanta on the pitmaster map with their incomparable Southern barbecue with a fiery Texas kick. Hearty portions of smoky beef bathed in a tangy tomato-based, vinegar-heavy sauce co-star alongside imaginative plates of chili-smothered "tater tots" and chicken fried ribs, which explains the long lines at this Candler Park hole-in-the-wall (and the fact that they were the second barbecue restaurant ever to be invited to cook at the James Beard House). But there are plenty of brews (over 50 bottles and 7 drafts) to console you while you wait. Or you can opt for their signature Bloody Mary—it's made with their house-made wing sauce, and the glass is even rimmed with their dry rub!

TASTE THE
LOVE

Frito Pie

(SERVES 8–10)

1 tablespoon olive oil (can substitute canola oil)
1 tablespoon unsalted butter
2 cups finely diced onion
¾ cup chopped jalapeños (can leave seeds intact for more spice)
2 tablespoons minced garlic
½ tablespoon kosher salt
1 teaspoon black pepper
1 (28-ounce) can crushed tomatoes
1½ tablespoons tomato paste
32 ounces beef stock (homemade preferred)
5 tablespoons chili powder
1½ tablespoons kosher salt
½ tablespoon granulated garlic powder
½ tablespoon granulated onion powder
½ tablespoon black pepper
½ tablespoon chipotle powder
½ tablespoon sugar
2 tablespoons adobo sauce from canned chipotles in adobo
¼ teaspoon ground cumin
2 tablespoons masa harina (corn flour)
1 cup warm water
1 pound chopped cooked brisket (recipe opposite)
14 (2-ounce) bags Fritos

In a heavy-bottomed, medium-size pot over medium heat, add the first seven ingredients (olive oil through 1 teaspoon black pepper). Sweat until the vegetables are tender, about 5 to 7 minutes. Add the next 12 ingredients (crushed tomatoes through cumin) and bring to a boil. Reduce the heat and simmer for 20 minutes.

Meanwhile, mix the masa harina and warm water together to make a slurry. Add the brisket to the pot, and mix in the slurry. Simmer for 5 to 10 minutes, stirring often. (*Note:* Do not to let the meat settle on the bottom.)

Cut open the bags of Fritos from the top or side and ladle the chili over Fritos. Optional: Garnish with shredded cheddar cheese, diced red onion, fresh sliced jalapeños, and a dollop of sour cream. Mix well and serve immediately.

Salt & Pepper Brisket

(SERVES 8–10)

1 (5-pound) bag hickory-wood chips, soaked in water for 1 to 3 hours
½ cup kosher salt
1 cup course black pepper
1 (8-pound) brisket flat

Preheat a smoker to 225°F. Apply the wood chips to allow for smoke.

Meanwhile, mix the kosher salt and black pepper together to make seasoning rub and apply it to the brisket. Place the brisket on the smoker, adding wood chips as necessary to supply ample smoke through cooking. Smoke the brisket until the internal temperature registers 170°F, about 4 to 7 hours. Remove the brisket and wrap in aluminum foil or butcher paper. Place the wrapped brisket back on the smoker. Continue cooking until the internal temperature reaches 190°F. Remove the brisket and allow to rest for 30 to 60 minutes.

Unwrap the brisket and and slice against the grain. Serve.

Chocolate Pecan Pie with Cinnamon Whipped Cream

(SERVES 8)

For the pie dough:

½ cup (1 stick) unsalted butter
2 cups all-purpose flour
¼ teaspoon salt
2 tablespoons sugar
¼ cup chilled club soda

For the chocolate mixture:

½ cup semisweet chocolate chips
2 tablespoons heavy cream
¼ teaspoon salt
½ teaspoon vanilla extract

For the pie filling:

1 cup light corn syrup
2 tablespoons melted unsalted butter
2 eggs, whisked
¼ cup light brown sugar, packed
¼ cup granulated sugar
1 teaspoon molasses
½ teaspoon salt
1½ teaspoons vanilla extract
1½ teaspoons cornstarch
2 tablespoons water
4 cups pecan halves

To make the pie dough: Cut the butter into 1-inch cubes and place in the freezer for 15 to 30 minutes. Meanwhile, in a bowl, combine the flour, salt, and sugar and mix well. Incorporate the cold butter into the flour mixture, pressing the flour and butter between your fingers until the flour resembles coarse crumbs. Slowly add the club soda, mixing until the dough begins to come together. Press and flatten the dough, wrap it in plastic wrap, and place in the refrigerator for at least 30 minutes.

To make the chocolate mixture: Pour the chocolate chips into a large glass bowl and place over a pot of simmering water. As the chips begin to melt, stir in the cream, salt, and vanilla until combined and smooth. Set aside.

To make the pie filling: In a bowl combine the corn syrup, melted butter, and whisked eggs, mixing well. Whisk in the brown sugar, granulated sugar, molasses, salt, and vanilla. In a separate bowl, dissolve the cornstarch in 2 tablespoons water to make a slurry. Add the slurry to the egg mixture. Whisk in the chocolate mixture until thoroughly combined.

To assemble the pie: Preheat the oven to 375°F. Roll the dough out until it's ¼-inch thick and roughly the size of a 9-inch pie pan. Place the dough into the pie pan, removing the excess around the edges. Place the pecan halves evenly into the shell. Pour the pie filling over the pecans and allow to settle for 5 minutes. Place the pie in the oven and bake until the center is set, about 55 to 60 minutes. Allow the pie to cool for at least 1 hour before serving.

Optional: Garnish with Cinnamon Whipped Cream (recipe opposite).

Cinnamon Whipped Cream

1 pint heavy cream
¼ cup confectioners' sugar
1 teaspoon vanilla extract
¼ teaspoon ground cinnamon

In a stand mixer, whisk heavy cream, confectioners' sugar, vanilla extract, and cinnamon until incorporated and the cream holds a stiff peak.

Gu's Bistro

5750 Buford Highway NE
Doraville, GA 30340
(770) 451-8118
gusbistro.com
Owner and Executive Chef: Yiquan Gu

Though Gu's Bistro is a family-owned, hole-in-the-wall Chinese joint tucked away in a drab shopping center, you won't find $5 fried rice on the menu. Instead, chile-laced dishes from Szechuan Province fill the tables, all made with high-quality ingredients, made-from-scratch sauces, and lots of love from chef Yiquan Gu, a native of Chengdu. Gu also uses a heavy hand to season his plates with numbing Szechuan peppercorns (he uses over 50 pounds every week)—an addictive sensation not often found in Atlanta, especially alongside craft beer (the restaurant has over seven options, including seasonal add-ins). The heat-averse will find comfort in the authentic tea-smoked duck, though more adventurous diners will revel in the Zhong Style Dumplings (Gu's wife makes nearly 200 every day by hand and is opening a dumpling shop at Krog Street Market) and mouthwatering *ma po* tofu. Beef fillet and tripe, a traditional staple of Szechuan cooking, is also fantastic, albeit a bit foreign to Western palates. Whatever you choose, you're sure to be charmed by the alluring decor—wooden model carts, red silk tapestries, and Chinese lanterns were all imported from China.

Dan Dan Noodles

(SERVE 2–3)

½ cup vegetable oil
1 cup ground beef
1 tablespoon yacai (preserved mustard greens)
½ cup chicken broth
1 tablespoon sesame paste
½ teaspoon sesame oil
1 teaspoon soy sauce
1 tablespoon red chili oil
½ teaspoon Szechuan peppercorn powder
2 cups egg noodles
1 cup snow pea leaves
1 teaspoon chopped scallions

Preheat a nonstick pan over medium-high heat for 2 minutes. Add the oil and ground beef and brown the beef until light brown, about 5 minutes. Add the yacai and stir-fry for 1 minute. Set aside.

In a medium saucepan over medium-high heat, bring the chicken broth to a boil. Add the boiling broth to a large serving bowl with the sesame paste, sesame oil, soy sauce, red chili oil, and Szechuan peppercorn powder.

In a large stockpot of boiling water, cook the noodles until soft, about 5 minutes. Drain and add the noodles to the broth mixture.

Blanch the snow pea leaves in hot water for 30 seconds. Drain and add to the broth mixture.

Add the beef to the broth mixture and mix well. Garnish with chopped scallions on top. Serve.

Ma Po Tofu

(SERVE 2–3)

1 (14-ounce) box soft tofu, cut into ¾-inch cubes
Pinch of salt
½ cup vegetable oil
⅔ cup ground beef
2 tablespoons black bean paste, chopped to smooth any large pieces
1 tablespoon chili powder
3 tablespoons Szechuan chili paste, chopped to smooth any large pieces
1 teaspoon soy sauce
1½ teaspoons Szechuan peppercorn powder, divided
1 cup chicken broth
⅛ cup leeks, cut into ¾-inch lengths
¼ cup green bean powder (available at Asian supermarkets)

Add 4 cups water, the tofu, and a pinch of salt to a large pot over medium-high heat, and bring to a boil. Drain and set the tofu aside.

Preheat a nonstick pan over medium-high heat for 2 minutes. Add the oil and ground beef and brown the beef until light brown, about 3 minutes. Add the black bean paste, chili powder, chili paste, soy sauce, and 1 teaspoon Szechuan peppercorn powder. Mix together. Add the chicken broth, leeks, and reserved tofu to the pot. Boil for 3 to 5 minutes.

Meanwhile, in a small bowl, combine the green bean powder with ¼ cup water. Add the mixture to the pot and boil for 1 minute.

Transfer mixture to a serving bowl and sprinkle the remaining ½ teaspoon Szechuan peppercorn powder over top. Serve.

Gunshow

924 Garrett Street
Atlanta, GA 30316
(404) 380-1886
gunshowatl.com

Owner: Kevin Gillespie
Executive Chef: Joey Ward

My first meal at Gunshow was one of the most fun, interactive, ballsy dining experiences I've had. I sat in the communal dining room, so spare it's practically undecorated, and watched as the chefs in the neighboring open kitchen worked their magic. I briefly wondered where the servers were, until I eyed chef Joey Ward, a Culinary Institute of America alum, heading my way. In his hands, he held a bowl of brussels sprouts drenched in a fragrant sauce. He told me the story behind his dish, how he made it, what it tasted like, and asked if I wanted to try it. Was there more than one answer to this question? This scenario repeated itself throughout the night, chefs coming from behind the stove, wielding carts and trays full of innovative dishes to our table, proffering them in a way that made it impossible to say no. I was glad we didn't—each dish was like nothing I've tasted before. I was intoxicated by the setup, which I later told owner Kevin Gillespie (of *Top Chef* fame) was the most brilliant marketing tactic I'd ever seen. He admitted the dim-sum-meets-churrascaria concept came to him after tiring of stuffy fine dining. "I wanted to offer the same quality ingredients and execution, but in a way that the people cooking could be the ones telling the story of the food," explains the Art Institute of Atlanta grad and former Woodfire Grill chef and co-owner. "Somebody reads a menu and says, 'I don't like beef tongue,' but when they see the dish and smell it and hear about it, suddenly they want it." It's true. I wanted everything that night, and again on my subsequent trips back to the East Atlanta destination. The energy is addicting—especially once I learned Gillespie writes his menu with the entire staff, down to the interns, every week. "Everyone has a say in what we produce—it's a wildly collaborative effort that helps newbies shape their voice in food and the older guys bask in new energy." No wonder *GQ* rated Gunshow one of the 12 Most Outstanding Restaurants of 2014. Bravo, chef!

Asher Bleu Grilled Cheese with Fennel Jam

(SERVES 8)

1 head fennel, cored and uniformly shredded in food processor to a thick sawdust consistency
½ (750-milliliter) bottle dry white wine
1 cup sugar
1 teaspoon salt
½ teaspoon fennel pollen (can substitute ground fennel seed)
5 ounces thinly sliced bleu cheese (Sweet Grass Dairy Asher Bleu preferred)
1 baguette sour-cherry pecan bread (Holeman & Finch preferred), sliced thin
½ cup (1 stick) softened unsalted butter

Combine the fennel, white wine, sugar, salt, and fennel pollen in a saucepan over medium heat. Reduce to jam-like consistency, about 20 minutes.

Place the bleu cheese evenly between 2 slices of bread. Butter the outsides of the bread. In a nonstick pan over medium-low heat, grill the sandwiches until the cheese in just melted and both sides are toasted, about 5 minutes per side. Serve with fennel jam.

Vietnamese-Style Chicken & Waffles

(SERVES 4)

4 tablespoons minced shallots
4 tablespoons minced ginger
2 tablespoons minced garlic
4 Thai bird chiles, minced
2 tablespoons sugar
1 teaspoon kosher salt
1 cup fish sauce (Red Boat or Squid preferred)
3 large limes, juiced
2 cups high-quality maple syrup
2 (8-ounce) chicken breasts, diced into 1-inch cubes
1 cup buttermilk
2 teaspoons monosodium glutamate (MSG; Ac´cent Flavor Enhancer preferred)
1 tablespoon kosher salt
1 cup all-purpose flour
⅓ cup cornstarch
⅓ cup rice flour
1 tablespoon kosher salt
1 teaspoon paprika
1 teaspoon black pepper
1 tablespoon garlic powder
1 tablespoon onion powder
1 gallon oil for frying (canola or peanut preferred)
Kosher salt to taste
Store-bought waffle batter (enough to make 2 waffles)
¾ cup roasted and chopped peanuts (can substitute pecans), plus ½ cup for garnish
2 tablespoons roughly chopped cilantro
4 tablespoons (½ stick) softened unsalted butter

Using a mortar and pestle, grind the first six ingredients (shallots through 1 teaspoon salt) to release the oils and dissolve the salt and sugar. (*Note:* If you don't have a mortar and pestle, you can use a blender instead.) Add the ground mixture to a large bowl. Mix in the fish sauce, lime juice, and maple syrup. Reserve.

Combine the chicken, buttermilk, MSG, and 1 tablespoon salt in a large bowl. Marinate for 1 hour in the refrigerator. Meanwhile, in a medium bowl, combine the next eight ingredients (all-purpose flour through onion powder), mixing well.

Heat the oil in a deep fryer until a candy thermometer reads 325°F. Remove the chicken from the marinade and dredge in the flour mixture. Carefully add the chicken to the hot oil and fry until golden and cooked through, about 6 minutes. Drain the fried chicken on paper towels and season lightly with kosher salt.

Meanwhile, make the waffle batter according to package directions. Add ¾ cup chopped peanuts to the batter, mixing well. Pour the batter onto a waffle maker set to medium-high and sprayed with nonstick pan spray. Bake until golden brown, about 4 minutes.

To serve, place the fried chicken on top of the waffles and drizzle with the syrup mixture. Garnish with the remaining ½ cup chopped peanuts, cilantro, and butter.

Kung Pao Brussels Sprouts

(SERVES 5)

1 gallon canola oil for frying (can substitute peanut oil)
30 brussel sprouts, quartered
Salt to taste
1 cup water
½ cup cornstarch
½ cup minced ginger
4 tablespoons minced garlic
6 tablespoons grapeseed oil
4 tablespoons sambal
1½ quarts soy sauce (Kikkoman preferred)
Splash of rice vinegar
1 cup sugar
1 cup chopped Szechuan chiles (can substitute any chile)
½ cup chopped peanuts

Heat the oil in a deep fryer until a candy thermometer reads 350°F. Carefully add the brussels sprouts to the hot oil and fry until golden brown, about 3 to 5 minutes. (*Note:* The brussels sprouts will pop, so stand back. If you don't have a deep fryer, you can roast the sprouts in a 400°F oven for 10 minutes instead.) Remove the sprouts from the oil and season with salt to taste.

Make a slurry by adding the water to cornstarch until it is the consistency of heavy cream.

For the kung pao sauce, in a small saucepan over medium heat, sweat the ginger and garlic in the grapeseed oil until fragrant, about 2 minutes. Add the sambal and sauté for 2 minutes. Add the soy sauce, vinegar, sugar, and chiles. (*Note:* Add water to balance out saltiness if needed.) Bring the mixture to a boil, then slowly add 1 cup of the slurry and simmer until the mixture coats the back of your spoon. Bring the mixture back to a boil, then remove from heat and cool to room temperature.

To serve, toss the fried brussels sprouts in the kung pao sauce and place them on a serving platter. Garnish with the chopped peanuts.

GARNISH & GATHER

"I always struggled with dinnertime—I was a busy working gal who wanted to eat local foods and cook at home, but I didn't always know how," says Atlanta native Emily Nethero Golub, who grew frustrated with CSAs and the obscure produce often found in their deliveries. "I really enjoyed the experience of exploring new fruits and veggies, but sometimes the amount of recipe planning, let alone grocery shopping and several jars of spices I'd only use once, got a little overwhelming." Certain she wasn't alone, Golub created Garnish & Gather, a gourmet recipe-kit meal service built from local, seasonal ingredients picked from nearby farms. It's the perfect dinnertime solution for busy Atlantans who love to cook and care about where the food comes from, but simply don't have time to plan their meals and grocery shop. There's even an extensive local market section where you can stock up on pantry staples like eggs, bread, coffee, milk, and snacks. The "Be the Chef" series is another great feature—the trailblazing company teams up with restaurants around the city to create special recipe kits (think St. Cecilia's famous octopus and Gunshow's killer shrimp and grits). "At the end of the day, you're supporting a local Atlanta business, a community of local farmers and food artisans, eating fresh and naturally grown produce, and feeling like a chef, all at the same time," says Golub. Sign me up!

Heirloom Market BBQ & Sobban

2243 Akers Mill Road
Atlanta, GA 30339
(770) 612-2502
heirloommarketbbq.com
Owners and Executive Chefs: Cody Taylor and Jiyeon Lee

1788 Clairmont Road
Decatur, GA 30033
(678) 705-4233
sobban.com
Owners and Executive Chefs: Cody Taylor and Jiyeon Lee

Southerners expect pulled pork sandwiches and mayo-laden coleslaw from their favorite barbecue joints. But local pork marinated in *gochujang* (Korean chile paste) alongside kimchee-spiked slaw is unprecedented. That was until Texas-born, Tennessee-raised, Atlanta-trained chef Cody Taylor traveled to Korea with his wife, Jiyeon Lee, a Korean teenage pop-star-turned-chef. Taylor kept noticing the similarities between Southern and Korean food, so the duo decided to turn this little piggie on its nose and comingle the two distinct cuisines into one revolutionary (and delicious!) style all their own. First at Heirloom Market BBQ, a roadside Southern barbecue joint employing Korean seasonings (if you

GARDEN GUN
Heirloom Market BBQ
Heirloom Market BBQ
Today's Specials
*Our "BLT" Sand w/side $9.50
*Rib Wingz w/side $10.50
*Texas Turkey Sand w/side $8.00
*Big Texas Sand w/side $8.00
HM Tacos and Smoked Wings on the Menu!!
Sides
*Green Tomato Kimchi
*Tempura Sweet Potato
*Cucumber Radish Salad
*Onion Rings
*Texas Beef Link $4.00
CHEDDARWURST
MISO BRATWURST
ANDOUILLE
ServSafe
CERTIFICATION
ZAGAT

NOW
AVAILABLE
HEIRLOOM
MARKET
BBQ
GIFT
CERTIFICATE

haven't tried the miso soup–injected brisket, you're missing out!) and most recently at Sobban, a Korean diner using Southern ingredients (their house-made tofu is a rarity in these parts). Both restaurants are laid-back with a vengeance: Sobban converted a former Arby's, while Heirloom is smaller than most one-bedroom apartments (read: standing room only, so to-go is your best bet). Both are inordinately cheap considering the quality and skill behind the dishes—"I don't think a lot of people realize the amount of work it takes," says Taylor, who arrives every day at 2 a.m. to fire up the smokers. "People don't see that, but barbecue is the longest-cooking fast food in the world, and it takes a lot of work."

Korean Pickled Green Tomatoes

(SERVES 4–6)

3 medium-size green tomatoes, sliced into 8 wedges
1 jalapeño, thinly sliced into rounds
2 small red radishes, shaved thin
1 cup rice vinegar
¼ cup sugar
3 teaspoons Korean red pepper flakes

In a large container with a lid, combine the green tomatoes, jalapeño, and radishes.

In separate mixing bowl, whisk together the rice vinegar, sugar, and Korean red pepper flakes until dissolved. Pour the pickling liquid over the vegetables and let sit at room temperature for 4 hours, covered. Place in refrigerator overnight. (*Note:* It's best if you can refrigerate these for 4 to 8 days.) Serve with grilled meats, barbecue, or on sandwiches.

Miso Collard Greens

(SERVES 4–6)

¼ pound (1 stick) unsalted butter
¼ cup vegetable oil
4 cloves garlic, minced
1 large Vidalia onion, cut into large dice
2 pounds collard greens, cleaned and cut into 2 x 2-inch pieces
½ cup vegetable stock
3 tablespoons Korean miso
1 tablespoon red pepper flakes
½ cup rice vinegar
Salt and pepper to taste

In large pot over medium-low heat, place the unsalted butter and vegetable oil. Once the butter is melted, stir in the garlic and onion and continue to sauté for 3 minutes. Add the collard greens, a few handfuls at a time, stirring and wilting slightly. Once all the collard greens have been added, mix in the vegetable stock, miso, red pepper flakes, and rice vinegar. Cover and reduce heat to low, cooking until tender and stirring occasionally, about 1 hour. Season with salt and pepper to taste. Serve as a side dish with any meal.

Pork with Peach Donkatsu

(SERVES 4)

4 boneless pork chops, pounded to ¼-inch thickness
½ cup sake
1 tablespoon salt
1 teaspoon black pepper
2 cups all-purpose flour
2 eggs, beaten with a splash of water
4 cups panko bread crumbs
Oil

For the peach donkatsu:

1 (15-ounce) can of peaches in heavy syrup
½ cup soy sauce
¼ cup sugar
¼ cup Worcestershire sauce
1 teaspoon black pepper

Marinate the pounded pork in the sake, salt, and pepper overnight.

The next day, drain the pork and dredge it in the flour. Dip the floured pork in the egg wash, letting any excess drip off. Dredge the pork in the panko. Chill in the refrigerator for at least 1 hour.

Heat the oil in a deep fryer until a candy thermometer reads 325°F. Carefully add the pork to the hot oil and fry until golden and cooked through, about 4 minutes, or until a thermometer registers 165°F. Drain the pork on paper towels and serve with peach donkatsu sauce.

To make the peach donkatsu sauce: Puree peaches and their syrup in a blender until smooth. Combine the puree with soy sauce, sugar, Worcestershire, and black pepper in a saucepan. Bring to a boil and then reduce heat to low and simmer until reduced by three-quarters, about 30 minutes.

White Oak Pastures

Peruse nearly any local grocery store's meat case and you're likely to find grass-fed beef from White Oak Pastures, a 145-year-old, 1,000-acre farm in south Georgia praised for its sustainable, humane practices. You'll likely also see the farm's pasture-raised chicken or free-range, organic eggs—the multigenerational family farm raises and hand-butchers 10 varieties of meat (cows, hogs, sheep, goats, rabbits, chickens, turkeys, guineas, ducks, and geese), not to mention pastured eggs and certified organic vegetables. "Atlanta is our home market—we are truly local and love the talented chefs that have given us so much support through the years and empowered us to reestablish the innovative animal welfare and environmental stewardship practices on our farm," says Will Harris, owner and chief farmer of White Oak Pastures (he's also president of the board of directors of Georgia Organics and beef director of the American Grassfed Association). You can also order White Oak products online (whiteoakpastures.com) or visit the farm to see for yourself just how special it truly is—there's even a restaurant and lodging cabins on-site.

Honey Pig

3473 Old Norcross Road, #304
Duluth, GA 30096
(770) 476-9292
honeypigatl.com
Owner: Wea Ju Lee
Executive Chef: Gio Park

One step into Honey Pig and you know an adventure awaits. The modern restaurant, an extension of a California chain that came to Atlanta's Korean-heavy Duluth neighborhood in 2007, offers Atlantans traditional Korean barbecue, where meats are grilled by the guest in domed cast-iron grills set in the center of the table. Bilingual servers are there to help the cooking-impaired, but it truly couldn't be easier (or more fun!). Go for the *sam-gyup-sal*, a perfectly marbled pork belly that melts in your mouth, or the jumbo tiger shrimp—they arrive shell-on, though your sever can help you deshell if needed. Purists will love the Kobe-style short ribs, sliced paper thin and ready within seconds. Complimentary snacks, like wasabi-marinated radishes, and wrappers (lettuce and rice paper) accompany all entrees, and in true Korean fashion, rice is served at the end of the meal. Wash it all down with soju, Korea's answer to sake with a hint of sweetness. How do you say "cheers" in Korean?

Kalbi

(SERVES 4)

- 1 cup packed brown sugar
- 2 pounds Korean-style ("flanken") beef short ribs
- 1 cup soy sauce
- ½ cup water
- ¼ cup mirin (rice wine)
- 1 small onion, peeled and finely grated
- 1 small Asian pear, peeled and finely grated
- 4 tablespoons minced garlic
- 2 tablespoons dark sesame oil
- ¼ teaspoon black pepper

Sprinkle the brown sugar over the beef and mix well to evenly coat. Let the beef sit at room temperature for 10 minutes.

Meanwhile, in a bowl, whisk together remaining ingredients. Transfer the beef into a large sealable freezer bag (you may need two) and add the marinade. Press out excess air from the bag; seal. Turn the bag over several times to ensure the beef is evenly coated. Refrigerate for at least 4 hours, preferably overnight.

Heat a gas or charcoal grill to medium-high. Remove the beef from the marinade and grill to desired doneness, about 3 to 4 minutes per side.

Optional: Garnish the beef with thinly sliced green onions, if desired. Serve whole pieces as a main course or cut into smaller pieces, using kitchen shears, for an appetizer.

Bibimbap

(SERVES 4)

For the sauce:

¾ cup gochujang (Korean spicy soybean paste)
6 tablespoons lemon-lime soda (Sprite preferred)
3 tablespoons doenjang (Korean soybean paste) or miso
2 tablespoons corn syrup
2 tablespoons sesame oil
2 tablespoons minced garlic
2 tablespoons minced ginger
1 tablespoons brown rice vinegar
1½ teaspoons sesame seeds

For the bibimbap:

4 ounces mung bean sprouts
8 ounces baby spinach
12 dried shiitake mushrooms
6 tablespoons canola oil, divided
3 teaspoons sesame oil, divided
2 tablespoons plus 2 teaspoons minced garlic, divided
2½ teaspoons minced ginger, divided
Kosher salt and black pepper to taste
6 ounces gosari (bracken fern), cut into 3-inch pieces
2 small Korean squash or zucchini, halved and cut crosswise into ¼-inch slices
2 medium carrots, julienned
¼ small daikon radish, julienned
¾ teaspoon sesame seeds, divided
8 ounces firm tofu, cut into ½-inch slabs
4 cups cooked white sushi rice
4 sunny-side-up eggs
2 leaves chicory, thinly sliced
2 leaves green-leaf lettuce, thinly sliced
1 scallion, thinly sliced

To make the sauce: In a medium bowl, whisk all of the ingredients together until smooth. Set aside.

To make the bibimbap: In a 4-quart saucepan, bring water to a boil. Add the sprouts and cook until crisp-tender, about 30 seconds. Transfer the sprouts to a bowl of ice water, drain, and dry with paper towels. Set aside.

Repeat the procedure with the spinach (squeeze out as much liquid as possible when draining). When finished, pour boiling water into a bowl and add the mushrooms; let soften for 30 minutes. Drain, remove stems, and slice ¼ inch thick. Set aside.

Heat 1 tablespoon canola oil and ½ teaspoon sesame oil in a 10-inch nonstick skillet over medium heat. Add 1 teaspoon garlic, ½ teaspoon ginger, and the softened mushrooms. Season with salt and pepper and cook until hot, about 2 minutes. Transfer the mushroom mixture to a bowl and set aside.

Repeat the procedure, using the same amounts of canola oil, sesame oil, garlic, and ginger, but this time adding the gosari, squash, carrot, and radish; season with salt and pepper. Set each aside in separate bowls, and add ¼ teaspoon sesame seeds to the radishes. Add 1½ teaspoons garlic, ¼ teaspoon sesame oil, salt, and pepper to both the sprouts and spinach; stir.

Heat the remaining canola oil in the skillet and add the tofu. Cook, turning once, until browned, about 4 to 6 minutes. Transfer the tofu to a plate and cut each slab in half.

To serve: Place 1 cup sushi rice in the center of each of four bowls, and top with an egg. Evenly divide the mushrooms in a mound in each bowl over the rice. Working clockwise, evenly portion the squash, carrot, radish, spinach, sprouts, gosari, chicory, and lettuce on top of the mushrooms. Place the tofu on the lettuces and sprinkle with sesame seeds and scallions. Serve with sauce on the side.

Little Italia

littleitalia.com

Owner and Executive Chef: Giovanni Di Palma

Antico Pizza Napoletano

1093 Hemphill Avenue
Atlanta, GA 30318
(404) 724-2333

Bar Amalfi

1099 Hemphill Avenue
Atlanta, GA 30318
(404) 724-2333

Bottega Luisa

1077 Hemphill Avenue
Atlanta, GA 30318
(404) 844-2707

Caffè Gio Gelateria Pasticceria

1093 Hemphill Avenue
Atlanta, GA 30318
(404) 724-2333

Gio's Chicken Amalfitano

1099 Hemphill Avenue
Atlanta, GA 30318
(404) 347-3874

Atlanta is known for many things—Coke, a killer aquarium, a mammoth airport, gorgeous trees, and juicy peaches, to name a few. But until recently, Atlanta and pizza would never be uttered in the same sentence, unless the words *mediocre* and *chain* were involved. That was until Giovanni Di Palma (Gio) came along—the Yankee took Atlanta by storm when he opened Antico Pizza Napoletana, a classic pizzeria using almost exclusively imported Italian ingredients. Since that fateful day in 2009, there's been a perpetual line around the block—no small feat considering the Home Park neighborhood was all but abandoned before Gio came into the picture. Hungry Atlantans would (and still do) wait for hours, vying for a taste of traditional Neapolitan pizza; once you try the sweet and spicy San Gennaro, pizza elsewhere may be ruined forever. Today, Antico is a production as much as a restaurant—chefs scramble around the open kitchen, swiping pies in and out of 1,000°F ovens anchoring the stark bakery-turned-even-barer-restaurant:

Communal tables outfitted with paper towels and jars of fresh garlic and peppers are the only conveniences afforded at Antico—they don't offer slices or delivery either.

But that hasn't stopped Gio from building a cultlike following, one that continues to proliferate as Gio continues transforming this rundown neighborhood of Midtown into his own Little Italy. To date, he's got a chicken-centric eatery (Gio's Chicken) highlighting the bright flavors of the Amalfi Coast; a panini and gelato shop (Caffè Gio) with a spacious patio; an Italian market (Bottega Luisa) selling imported olive oils, pastas, and tomatoes alongside fresh antipasti; and an open-air limoncello bar (Bar Amalfi) that wouldn't be out of place in Salerno. *Grazie*, Gio. You've given Atlanta a slice of Italy we'd normally need a transcontinental plane ticket to experience.

Chicken Zuppa

(SERVES 8)

2 tablespoons olive oil
6 cloves garlic, chopped
3 ribs celery, chopped
3 carrots, chopped
1 onion, chopped
Salt to taste
2 quarts chicken stock
Pepper to taste
1 tablespoon fresh oregano, chopped
1 (3–3½-pound) roasted chicken
½ pound pastina (can substitute any small noodles)

In a deep medium-size pot, combine the olive oil, garlic, celery, carrots, and onion. Season with salt and sauté until the onions are translucent, about 3 minutes. Deglaze the pan with the chicken stock and bring to a boil. Reduce the heat to a simmer, season with salt, pepper, and oregano.

Add the whole roasted chicken to the pot until it's completely submerged. Cook for 20 minutes, then remove the chicken, pull off the meat, and shred it with two forks. Put the pulled chicken back into the soup. Simmer for 30 minutes, skimming the foam or excessive oil from the top.

In a medium pot, bring 2 quarts salted water to a boil. Drop the pastina into the boiling water and cook until al dente, about 7 minutes. Remove the pastina, drain, and rinse in cold water.

To serve, spoon 2 ladlesful of the rinsed pastina into the bottom on a bowl. Pour enough soup over top to nearly fill the bowl.

Optional: Garnish with chopped Italian parsley and Pecorino Romano.

Chicken Scarpiello

(SERVES 4)

1 (3-pound) whole chicken
Sea salt and black pepper to taste
Granulated garlic to taste
2 tablespoons olive oil, divided
1 teaspoon chopped garlic
8 Italian sausages
¼ cup cipolline onions
¼ cup dolce picante peppers (can substitute sweet cherry peppers)
2 tablespoons red wine vinegar
2 tablespoons white wine
Pinch each of salt and pepper
Pinch of fresh oregano
8 tablespoons chicken stock

Trim the fat from the chicken and cut it in half, removing the backbone. Season the chicken with sea salt, black pepper, and granulated garlic, and drizzle 1 tablespoon olive oil over top. Roast the chicken, uncovered, at 375°F for 30 minutes. Once the chicken has cooled, chop the meat into medium-size pieces and set aside.

Add the remaining 1 tablespoon olive oil to a oven-safe sauté pan over medium heat. Add the garlic, sausage, onions, and peppers and brown them, about 4 minutes. Deglaze the pan with the red wine vinegar, reduce heat to low, and reduce by half, about 3 minutes. Add the white wine, salt, pepper, and oregano. Increase the heat to high and add the chicken pieces and chicken stock, basting with the white wine sauce as it cooks, about 1 minute. Place the sauté pan under the broiler for 3 minutes.

To plate, transfer the chicken pieces to a large plate. Pour the sauce and peppers over the chicken. Serve.

Miller Union

999 Brady Avenue NW
Atlanta, GA 30318
(678) 733-8550
millerunion.com
Executive Chef and Co-Owner: Steven Satterfield
General Manager and Co-Owner: Neal McCarthy

Steven Satterfield, a Savannah native, didn't start cooking seriously until he was 30. Shocking, considering the slew of awards he's got under his belt—*Food & Wine*'s "People's Best New Chef," *Bon Appétit*'s and *Esquire*'s "Best New Restaurants in America," *Atlanta* magazine's "Restaurant of the Year," and three James Beard nominations, to name a few. Satterfield's trajectory is unlike most chefs': He graduated from Georgia Tech's architecture program and was the lead guitarist in the award-winning band Seely for six years. But between tours he needed pocket money, so he convinced Anne Quatrano to hire him as a line cook at Floataway Café, and then Scott Peacock at the original Watershed. Naturally, Satterfield started dreaming of opening his own place, and in 2009, his dream became a reality. "Nothing was opening then and people called us crazy, but it turned out we were a breath of fresh air during a really depressing time." Satterfield's Miller Union, located in a revamped warehouse for the former stockyards, was indeed restorative. A shameless love letter to local produce, it's a refined, farm-driven spot with just a hint of a Southern accent (see the legendary farm egg baked in celery cream), a place where in-season vegetables call the shots and serve as the foundation of nearly every dish, each of which is perfectly paired with co-owner, general manager, and certified sommelier Neal McCarthy's wine list, a collection of small producers focused on Old World, biodynamic, and organic varietals. Equally impressive: Half the staff are certified sommeliers (McCarthy and Satterfield paid for their certifications).

Peach, Arugula & Greek Yogurt Salad

(SERVES 4)

For the yogurt:

¼ cup sheep's milk brebis (can substitute ricotta cheese or goat's milk chèvre)
½ cup whole milk Greek yogurt
½ teaspoon lemon zest
1 tablespoon lemon juice
1 tablespoon honey
1 pinch fine sea salt

For the salad:

3 cups ripe peaches, peeled, pitted, and sliced
1 tablespoon chopped mint
1 tablespoon chopped basil
1 tablespoon chopped sorrel
2 bunches arugula
1½ teaspoons lemon juice
3 teaspoons extra-virgin olive oil
Salt and pepper to taste

To make the yogurt: In a medium bowl, whisk together the brebis, yogurt, lemon zest and juice, honey, and salt until combined.

To make the salad: Divide the yogurt mixture among four bowls.

In a medium bowl, combine the peaches, herbs, arugula, lemon juice, olive oil, and salt and pepper. Toss to combine and adjust for seasoning. Place the peach mixture on top of the yogurt mixture. Serve.

Fall Squash & Mushroom Ragout with Citrus-Scented Grits

(SERVES 4)

1 large butternut squash, peeled, seeded (reserve seeds), and cut into 1-inch cubes
1 red onion, diced
½ teaspoon roughly chopped thyme leaves
½ teaspoon roughly chopped rosemary leaves
½ teaspoon roughly chopped sage leaves
¼ cup extra-virgin olive oil
1 tablespoon kosher salt
1 teaspoon freshly ground pepper
¼ cup kosher salt
4 cups mixed mushrooms, trimmed (reserve stems and scraps) and torn into bite-size pieces
1 tablespoon minced fresh garlic
1 tablespoon finely diced shallot
4 tablespoons extra-virgin olive oil
2 teaspoons salt, plus more as needed
1 teaspoon freshly ground pepper, plus more as needed
1 shallot
1 small carrot
1 rib celery
1 sprig thyme
2 pieces dried porcini mushroom
2 cups water
2 cups milk
1½ teaspoons kosher salt
1 cup stone-ground white grits
½ cup heavy cream
4 tablespoons unsalted butter
Zest of a bitter orange (can substitute chopped kumquat)

Preheat oven to 375°F. Toss the first 8 ingredients in a large bowl and stir to combine. Transfer to a parchment-lined sheet pan and roast until squash is tender, about 20 to 25 minutes.

Combine 4 cups cool water with ¼ cup kosher salt and stir to dissolve. Add the reserved squash seeds and let sit for at least 30 minutes. Drain well, but do not rinse. Arrange the seeds in a single layer on a cookie sheet.

Once the squash is done roasting, lower the oven temperature to 300°F. Roast the seeds, stirring from time to time, until crisp and golden brown, about 20 minutes. Remove and allow to cool. When cool, pulse the roasted seeds in a blender or food processor to roughly chop. Set aside.

Increase oven temperature to 400°F. In a large bowl, toss the mixed mushrooms with the garlic, shallot, olive oil, salt, and pepper. Transfer the mushroom mixture to a sheet pan and spread out evenly. Roast until slightly browned but not crisp, about 10 to 12 minutes.

In a medium saucepan, add the reserved mushroom stems and scraps, shallot, carrot, celery, thyme sprig, and dried porcinis. Add water just to cover and simmer until the broth darkens, about 25 minutes. Strain out the solids, season with salt and pepper to taste, and set aside.

In a heavy saucepan over low heat, combine the water, milk, and 1½ teaspoons salt and bring to a simmer. Add the grits and stir constantly until the grits tighten up. When the grits are tender, add the cream and butter and season to taste. Stir in the zest.

To serve, evenly divide the cooked grits into the bottom of four shallow bowls. Add ½ cup roasted butternut squash to each bowl. Divide the roasted mushrooms among the bowls. Add a spoonful of the reserved mushroom broth to each bowl, then garnish with the chopped toasted squash seeds.

Optional: Top with a fried sage leaf.

One Eared Stag

1029 Edgewood Avenue NE
Atlanta, GA 30307
(404) 525-4479
oneearedstag.com
Owner and Executive Chef: Robert Phalen

The food world is going through a renaissance of sorts when it comes to ingredients, and I don't mean local and seasonal. I'm talking about uncommon, undervalued cuts of meat that minimize waste, enhance flavor, and give diners something new. Now when I eat out, my eyes leapfrog over the fillet and sprint toward pâté, collar, cheek, and, of course, foie. Leading the charge in Atlanta is Robert Phalen, chef-owner of Inman Park's charming One Eared Stag. One glance at his menu—beef heart pastrami, fried chicken necks, roasted tuna collar, and Bolognese made from pig's feet—and I was hooked. "Sure, it's a financial decision, but really I'm just a family man, and my approach to running a restaurant goes back to getting my kids to eat things like tongue," explains Phalen, who butchers whole animals in-house, scrapes fish from the bones for tartare, and sources most of his products from within 100 miles of the restaurant. "If I put tongue in tomato sauce and they like it, then we've done it. You can't necessarily taste the difference, but we're a no-waste kitchen using a product that's less expensive and equally, if not more, delicious." Vegetarians don't get shortchanged either—a celery salad with endive and apple is one of my favorite dishes on Phalen's constantly evolving menu. And you're not resigned to pig's feet alone. Less-experimental diners will still be wowed by Phalen's creamy shrimp and grits, crispy fried chicken, melty grilled cheese, and the illustrious Meatstick (a double-stack burger infused with bacon). Even better? None of the small plates exceeds $19, so take my advice and share a round with a group. And don't overlook brunch—"it's not overcooked eggs, tiny potatoes, and bacon cooked to no end," assures Phalen, whose eggs are always fluffy and topped with caviar.

Celery & Apple Salad

(SERVES 5)

½ cup extra-virgin olive oil
¼ cup plus 2 tablespoons raw peanuts, divided
½ árbol chile, seeded and minced
4 teaspoons lemon juice
3 tablespoons Champagne vinegar
1 teaspoon kosher salt, plus more to taste
½ teaspoon freshly ground pepper, plus more to taste
1 bunch celery, sliced
2 endives, sliced
1 Jonagold apple, sliced
1½ cup shredded Manchego cheese
¼ cup Italian parsley leaves
1 shallot, diced
2 tablespoons chopped chives
¼ cup lovage
¼ cup buckwheat flowers

In a small pot over low heat, add the olive oil and ¼ cup peanuts and cook until warm, about 5 minutes. Place the warm peanuts and oil in a food processor and pulse until roughly chopped. Immediately pour the peanut mixture into a small bowl with the árbol chile, and let sit for 10 minutes. Add the lemon juice, vinegar, 1 teaspoon kosher salt, and ½ teaspoon ground pepper. Whisk to combine and set aside.

In a large bowl, combine remaining ingredients, seasoning with salt and pepper to taste. Dress with peanut vinaigrette, toss, garnish with remaining 2 tablespoons peanuts, and serve.

Broccoli & Gruyère Soup

(SERVES 5–6)

½ pound (2 sticks) unsalted butter
1 large sweet onion, diced
1 carrot, diced
2 garlic cloves, minced
3 bunches broccoli
4 cups chicken stock
2 fresh bay leaves
1 teaspoon cayenne pepper
½ teaspoon smoked paprika
1 cup shredded gruyère cheese
2 cups heavy cream
Salt to taste

In a large sauce pot over medium heat melt the butter. Add the onions, carrot, and garlic, and sweat until the onions are translucent, about 10 minutes. Add the broccoli (stalks and florets), discarding the woody ends, and sauté for 5 minutes. Pour the chicken stock over the broccoli to cover. Add the bay leaves, cayenne pepper, and paprika. Reduce heat to low and simmer until the broccoli is tender, about 15 to 20 minutes. Add the gruyère and heavy cream, and simmer for 5 to 10 minutes longer. Transfer the soup to a food processor and blend until smooth. Season with salt to taste. Serve immediately.

Dirty Farro

(SERVES 5–6)

2 cups farro
2 bay leaves
1 sprig thyme
2 garlic cloves
3 shallots
1 tablespoon unsalted butter
1 clove garlic, sliced
½ top of knob (or spring) onion, sliced
½ cup pureed pastured chicken liver
Salt to taste
1 bunch beet greens, cleaned and chopped
A lot of cracked black pepper

In a large pot over medium heat, simmer the farro with the aromatics (bay leaves through shallots) until the grain pops, about 20 minutes. Drain the farro and cool.

Meanwhile, in a sauté pan over medium heat, melt the butter with the garlic and onions for 1 minute. Add the livers and season with salt to taste. Cook for 5 minutes, then add the popped farro. Season with salt and mix well. Cook for another 5 minutes, allowing the farro to slightly fry. Add the beet greens, let wilt slightly, and season with black pepper. Serve immediately.

ONE FLEW SOUTH

6000 North Terminal Parkway
Atlanta, GA 30320
(404) 816-3464
ONEFLEWSOUTHATL.COM
Owners: Jackmont Hospitality Inc. and Global Concessions Inc.
Executive Chef: Duane Nutter
Master Mixologist: Tiffanie Barriere

Fast food, chain restaurants, sad sandwich kiosks. This is what the majority of airport dining looks like. Not so at Hartsfield-Jackson, thanks to a sophisticated spot in the international concourse called One Flew South. Since 2008, this chef-driven restaurant helmed by Seattle-native Duane Nutter, who hails from Louisville's AAA Five-Diamond Oakroom, has been dazzling travelers with a Southern-based, globally inspired menu (think duck confit sandwiches, thyme-roasted pork belly with black-eyed pea salad, and house-cured salmon bruschetta) in the most unsuspecting of locales. It's no easy feat—the *Iron Chef America* star has to bring every single item through TSA inspection, not to mention having all 17 knives chained to the counter and passing three annual inspections (city health, airport, and a knife inspection). "The knife thing is tough, but my biggest hurdle is that anyone who delivers product to the airport must have a $10 million insurance policy, so I can't call just anyone," says Nutter. "The logistics can be a pain, but my satisfied guests are worth it—you wouldn't think we'd have regulars, but we have people who come in every Thursday for a drink, diners who miss their flights to keep eating, and guests who schedule layovers solely to come eat here." One bite of Nutter's bacon BLT with black truffle mayo, and I understand.

Smoked Trout Potato Salad

(SERVES 4)

1 (8-ounce) pack smoked trout, skin removed, roughly chopped
1 cup medium-dice peeled sweet potatoes, blanched
½ bunch chopped Italian parsley
1½ cups blanched peas (Cimino Farm preferred), some water saved
4 tablespoons olive oil
Zest of 2 lemons
Black pepper to taste
1 boiled egg, peeled and cut into 4 wedges

Combine the trout in a large mixing bowl with the sweet potatoes, parsley, half of the blanched peas, olive oil, and lemon zest. Season with black pepper to taste and mix well.

Place the remaining blanched peas in a blender with enough water from blanching to pulse into a smooth puree.

Divide the trout and potato salad into four bowls. Add an egg wedge and a spoonful of the pea puree to each bowl. Serve with your favorite crackers.

Pineapple "Not Upside Down" Cake

(SERVES 16)

1 (15-ounce) can pumpkin puree
4 eggs
1 cup vegetable oil
⅔ cup water
3 cups brown sugar
3½ cups all-purpose flour
2 teaspoons baking soda
1½ teaspoons salt
1 teaspoon ground cinnamon
1 teaspoon ground nutmeg
½ teaspoon ground cloves
¼ teaspoon ground ginger
2 pineapples, peeled, quartered, and cored
1 cup bourbon
3 (6-ounce) cans pineapple juice
1 vanilla bean, split
3 tablespoons cornstarch
3 tablespoons water
Unsalted butter

Preheat the oven to 350°F. Grease and flour two 8½ x 4 x 2½-inch loaf pans.

In a large bowl, mix the pumpkin puree, eggs, oil, water, and brown sugar until well blended.

In a separate bowl, whisk the flour, baking soda, salt, cinnamon, nutmeg, cloves, and ginger until thoroughly combined.

Stir the dry ingredients into the pumpkin mixture until just blended. Pour the mixture into the prepared pans. Bake until a toothpick inserted in the center comes out clean, about 50 minutes.

Once the cake is done, decrease the oven temperature to 325°F. Meanwhile, in a large oven-safe sauté pan over medium heat, sear the pineapple until golden brown on both sides, about 3 minutes per side. Deglaze the pan with the bourbon, pineapple juice, and vanilla bean. Cover the pan with foil and bake until fork tender, about 40 minutes. Meanwhile, combine the cornstarch and water and mix until smooth. Set aside. (*Note:* This is the slurry.)

Remove the pineapple, reserving the liquid, and set aside to cool. Pour the liquid into a saucepan over medium-high heat. Remove the vanilla bean pod, add the slurry, and bring to a boil until the liquid is slightly thickened and coats the back of a spoon.

To serve, cut each loaf into 8 slices. Lightly butter both sides of each slice and place on a grill preheated to high; cook until the milk solids are charred, about 2 minutes per side. Serve immediately, drizzling each slice with the bourbon-braised pineapple and the sauce.

Panahar

3375 Buford Highway NE
Atlanta, GA 30329
(404) 633-6655
panaharbangladeshi.com

Co-Owner and Executive Chef: Mohammed Khurshid Alam
Co-Owner: Mustafa Mahmud

The year 2001 welcomed the first Bangladeshi restaurant to Atlanta, an unassuming spot hidden in an unremarkable strip mall on Buford Highway. For as modest as it looks, the food, so bright and flavorful, is proportionately extraordinary. Chef and co-owner Mohammed Khurshid Alam, who doesn't use any curry powder and makes all condiments, spice blends, cheese, and yogurt in-house, turns out authentic dishes from his native Noakhali that are significantly less oily and spicy than the Indian flavors you're likely used to. Though the chicken tikka *moshala* is most popular, you'll be pleasantly surprised if you order the vegetarian-friendly *halim* soup or the lamb korma cooked in a turmeric-laced cream sauce with chopped almonds and raisins. Or the fish *dopiazza*—fillets are sautéed in a black-mustard-heavy sauce draped with grilled onions and cilantro. Don't forget to BYOB—Panahar doesn't even charge a corkage fee.

Dharosh Bhaaji

(Sautéed Okra)

(SERVES 2)

1 tablespoon canola oil
½ medium onion, thinly sliced
2 pounds fresh okra, cut into ¼-inch slices
½ tomato, thinly sliced
½ teaspoon turmeric powder
½ tablespoon minced garlic

Heat the oil in a large sauté pan over medium-high heat. Add the onions and sauté for 1 minute. Add the okra, sauté for 1 minute, and reduce heat to medium. Cover and cook until the okra has softened, about 2 to 3 minutes. Add the tomatoes, turmeric, and garlic and stir until mixed well. Serve with white rice.

Buford Highway

New York has Little Italy; Los Angeles, Chinatown. Atlanta, though lacking these micro-neighborhoods, has Buford Highway, a 26-mile cornucopia of international eats. The constantly evolving amalgamation of restaurants (there are more than 1,000) are almost always immigrant-owned, family-operated holes-in-the-wall found in unprepossessing strip malls, or in other words, incredibly authentic and delicious. The food is also insanely cheap. A banh mi (a Vietnamese sandwich often stuffed with pork and pickled vegetables) will run you just $2.50 at the celebrated Lee's Bakery, and it may just be the best sandwich you've ever had. If not, there's a dozen other Vietnamese bakeries, and pho parlors, to choose from. I'm partial to Pho Dai Loi #2, where the steaming hot bowls of cardamom-spiked broth come chock-full of tender beef, chewy noodles, and more herbs than you'll know what to do with, and Nam Phuong, whose fish-sauce-glazed chicken wings and BBQ pork make-it-yourself spring rolls are bursting with lick-your-fingers flavor.

Peppered between these is a boatload of other Asian cuisines (hence the highway's nickname, "Chambodia"), from dim sum (Canton House is a local favorite) to Szechuan (you'll find fiery recipes from Gu's Bistro on page 114) to Korean barbecue (check out Woo Nam Jeong Stone Bowl for intensely flavored *bulgogi* and bibimbap). There's also a healthy portion of Latin options, like beef-tongue tacos on house-made tortillas at Taqueria El Rey, and the best fish tacos in town at El Señor Taco (where you'll also find incredible handmade *sopes*). Flip to page 149 for a flavorful recipe from Atlanta's first Bangladeshi restaurant, Panahar. Whichever gem you pick, rest assured your taste buds will thank you.

Ron Eyester

Owner and Executive Chef: Ron Eyester

Rosebud

1397 North Highland Avenue NE
Atlanta, Georgia 30306
(404) 347-9747
rosebudatlanta.com
Chef de Cuisine: Christian Rodriguez

The Family Dog

1402 North Highland Avenue NE
Atlanta, GA 30306
(404) 249-0180
thefamilydogatlanta.com
Partner: Jason Chenette

Timone's

1409 North Highland Avenue NE, Suite D
Atlanta, GA 30306
(404) 809-2979
timonespizzaatlanta.com
Managing Partner and Bar Director: Jason Kemp
Partner: Jason Chenette

We've come to expect seasonal-only dishes at fine-dining restaurants (as in, no tomatoes in December or brussels sprouts in July), but our standards aren't usually as high at casual eateries. Ron Eyester is changing that at his three Morningside restaurants, all of which adhere to one simple rule: Buy local. Make that two simple rules: Buy local and play good music. The chef admittedly devotes as much time to his playlists as he does to the reinvented Southern classics he serves at Rosebud, a clamorous neighborhood restaurant named for Jerry Garcia's guitar. Though not a formally trained chef, Eyester's trifecta of restaurants are insanely popular—brunch at Rosebud is practically an institution, and The Family Dog, named for the infamous music collective in San Francisco, affords the neighborhood a watering hole like no other, complete with innovative cocktails, craft beer, and elevated pub fare like lobster egg rolls. Eyester returned to his roots when he opened Timone's, a local pizza joint paying tribute to his Long Island upbringing, and he broke into Atlantic Station with a diner concept plainly called Diner. Though there's nothing plain about Eyester, who's known as "the Angry Chef" for his rants on Twitter ("If you want to create your own entree, I might suggest a grocery store and cooking classes," one such Tweet read). That zing's as strong as his beloved Bloody Mary!

Rosebud's Wild Georgia Shrimp & Grits

(SERVES 6)

4 tablespoons unsalted butter, divided
2 cups thinly sliced Vidalia onion
1½ cups half-and-half, plus more if needed
3¼ cups chicken broth, divided, plus more if needed
1½ cups stone-ground grits (Riverview Farms recommended)
½ teaspoon granulated garlic
½ teaspoon sugar
Kosher salt and freshly ground pepper to taste
1 tablespoon finely chopped garlic
1 cup chopped andouille sausage
1 (14-ounce) can chopped San Marzano tomatoes
½ pound fresh Georgia shrimp, peeled and deveined
¼ cup finely assorted herbs (oregano, thyme, marjoram, and parsley)

In a large, straight-sided sauté pan, heat 2 tablespoons butter over medium heat and swirl to coat the bottom of the pan. Add the onions and cook until softened, about 5 minutes. Reduce the heat to low and let the onions cook, stirring only occasionally, until they have caramelized, about 10 to 12 minutes.

In a large saucepan over medium-high heat, bring the half-and-half and 2 cups chicken broth to a simmer. Gradually whisk in the grits and return to a boil. Reduce the heat to low and cook the grits until soft and creamy with just a little bite, about 30 minutes, stirring often to prevent scorching. If the grits become too thick, add a little more half-and-half or broth. Season the grits with the granulated garlic, sugar, and salt and pepper to taste.

While the grits are cooking, add the chopped garlic to the caramelized onions and increase the heat to medium-high. Cook until the garlic is fragrant, about 1 minute. Scrape the onion mixture to the side of the pan and add the sausage. Let the sausage cook for an additional 5 to 7 minutes, turning to brown on both sides. Add the tomatoes and the remaining 1¼ cups chicken broth and bring to a boil. Reduce the heat to low and let the mixture reduce and thicken, about 10 minutes. Add the shrimp and cook just until curled and opaque, about 4 minutes. Stir in the remaining 2 tablespoons butter, herbs, and salt and pepper to taste.

To serve, divide the grits evenly among six plates. Top with the shrimp and spoon broth over the top.

The Family Dog's Ginger Jump

(SERVES 1)

2 ounces white whiskey (American Spirit Whiskey preferred)
1 ounce creme de violette
½ ounce fresh lemon juice
Ice
Ginger beer
Drop of lavender bitters
Fresh mint sprig

Combine the first three ingredients (whiskey through lemon juice) in a cocktail shaker with ice. Shake and pour into an iced collins glass.

Top with the ginger beer and lavender bitters. Garnish with the mint sprig.

Timone's Meatballs in Red Sauce

(SERVES 10–12)

For the meatballs:

2 yellow onions, grated
2 fennel bulbs, grated
5 garlic cloves, minced
4 tablespoons olive oil
1 cup white wine
1 cup chopped Italian parsley
3 cups grated Romano cheese
5 cups panko bread crumbs
5 egg yolks
1¼ cups crushed San Marzano tomatoes
1 teaspoon red pepper flakes
Salt and pepper to taste
2½ pounds ground beef (Riverview Farms preferred)
2½ pounds ground pork (Riverview Farms preferred)
3 quarts soybean oil (can substitute canola oil)

For the red sauce:

1¼ tablespoons olive oil (local preferred)
¼ pound (1 stick) unsalted butter
2 onions, chopped
1 stalk celery, chopped
2 carrots, chopped
Salt and pepper to taste
12 cloves garlic, chopped
½ cup chopped oregano
2 tablespoons red pepper flakes
4 quarts pureed San Marzano tomatoes
¼ cup chopped fresh basil

To make the meatballs: Use a rondo or some sort of round sauté pan with a 3-inch lip to keep from spilling over the sides. It will take about 10 minutes to caramelize the vegetables.

In a round sauté pan over medium-high heat, sauté the onion, fennel, and garlic in olive oil for about 10 minutes. Deglaze the pan with white wine.

In a large bowl combine the cooked onion mixture with the parsley, cheese, bread crumbs, egg yolks, tomatoes, red pepper flakes, salt, pepper, ground beef, and ground pork. Spread the mixture onto sheet pan, covered with plastic wrap and chill in the refrigerator for at least 3 hours, or overnight if possible.

Using a 2½-ounce scoop, portion meatballs out of the chilled meat mixture and set on a sheet pan. Chill the meatballs in the refrigerator for at least 1 hour (overnight is preferred).

Heat the oil in a heavy-bottomed pot or a deep fryer until a candy thermometer registers 300°F. Carefully lower the meatballs into the hot oil in batches of 6 to 10, depending on the pot size, and fry until the outside of the meatball has browned, about 90 seconds.

To make the red sauce: Add the olive oil and butter to a dutch oven over medium heat. When just melted but not browned, add the onions, celery, and carrots and season with salt and pepper. Sweat until translucent, about 3 minutes. Add the garlic, oregano, and red pepper flakes, and sweat for 3 minutes. Add the pureed tomatoes and stir to combine. Bring the sauce to a simmer and continue to cook until the sauce is reduced by one-third. Puree the reduced sauce in a food processor until smooth. Add the fresh basil and adjust seasoning if necessary.

To finish: Add the fried meatballs to the tomato sauce and cook for 2½ hours over moderate heat.

Serpas Restaurant

659 Auburn Avenue NE #501
Atlanta, GA 30312
(404) 688-0040
serpasrestaurant.com

Owner and Executive Chef: Scott Serpas
Sous Chef: Manuel Lara

The first time I met chef Scott Serpas, I had to ask him to repeat himself after most sentences. The New Orleans native has an accent so thick, I was shocked to learn he's been cooking in Atlanta for more than a decade. First at now-shuttered Nava (a Buckhead Life restaurant) and then at Sia's, Mitra, and as the opening chef at TWO urban licks (Serpas is responsible for those legendary salmon chips). Today, he's running his first eponymous restaurant, Serpas, housed in a historical cotton storage factory circa the 1900s. The sexy industrial space has all the ingredients for a successful Atlanta restaurant: Historical tie-in? Check (see the sweeping mural of a cotton

blossom). Exposed brick, reclaimed wood, concrete floors? Check. Spacious outdoor patio? Check. Delicious food? Check. Serpas's Old Fourth Ward hideaway dishes up approachable cuisine with a flicker of Louisiana panache hobnobbing with Southwestern and Asian flavors (from his time at Nava and Sia's, respectively). Though I'm smitten with his fried oysters, so perfectly balanced with bright pickled chiles, the Creole-style brunch is equally drool-worthy. Don't miss his bona fide beignets and andouille-style pigs in a blanket.

Tuna Tartare

(SERVES 2–4)

¼ cup Sriracha sauce
½ cup rice vinegar
1 tablespoon toasted sesame seeds
1 tablespoon sugar
1 teaspoon salt
Juice of 1 lemon
6 tablespoons sesame oil
6 ounces sushi-grade yellowfin tuna, medium dice
1 tablespoon finely diced red onion
4 tablespoons finely diced green apple
10 cilantro leaves, torn
1 avocado, diced small
Salt to taste

Mix the first six ingredients (Sriracha through lemon juice) together in a large bowl. Slowly pour a stream of oil into the mixture while whisking until incorporated. Set aside.

Add the remaining ingredients (tuna through salt) to a medium serving bowl. Toss to combine. Dress with Sriracha vinaigrette and toss until completely coated. Serve with your favorite chips.

Flash-Fried Oysters

(SERVES 3–4)

For the pickled mirliton:

1 mirliton (can substitute celery or jicama)
3 tablespoons diced red onion
1 Anaheim chile, seeded and sliced into thin rings
½ teaspoon minced garlic
3 tablespoons white vinegar
5 tablespoons olive oil
Salt and pepper to taste

For the Creole tartar sauce:

2 cups mayonnaise
¼ cup finely diced red onion
Juice of 1 lemon
3 tablespoons Creole mustard
3 tablespoons sugar
2 teaspoons capers
Salt to taste

For the oysters:

1½ cups corn flour
2 teaspoons chili powder
2 teaspoons cayenne pepper
1 teaspoon onion powder
1 teaspoon garlic powder
2 tablespoon cornstarch
3 tablespoons kosher salt
1 dozen shucked Gulf oysters
1½ quarts canola oil for frying

To make pickled mirliton: Boil 1 mirliton in a pot filled with water for 25 minutes. Peel and dice the cooked mirliton and add to a glass bowl. Add red onion, chile, garlic, white vinegar, and olive oil. Fold all ingredients together and season with salt and pepper to taste. Marinate for 4 hours.

To make the Creole tartar sauce: Combine mayonnaise, red onion, lemon juice, Creole mustard, sugar, and capers in a nonreactive bowl. Whisk ingredients together and season with salt to taste.

To make the oysters: Mix the first seven ingredients (corn flour through salt) together in a large bowl. Dredge the oysters through the seasoned corn flour.

In a heavy-bottomed pot or deep fryer, heat the oil to 350°F. Carefully add the oysters to the hot oil and fry for 1 minute. Remove the oysters and place on paper towels to drain. Arrange oysters on a plate and garnish with Creole tartar sauce and pickled mirliton.

Seven Lamps

3400 Around Lenox Road NE #217
Atlanta, GA 30326
(404) 467-8950
sevenlampsatl.com
Owner and Executive Chef: Drew Van Leuvan

Atlanta is full of comestible surprises, from the hidden gems on Buford Highway to the incredible spots squirreled away in seemingly forsaken neighborhoods. But Seven Lamps may be my favorite diamond in the rough. Camouflaged in the corner of a chain-littered shopping center neighboring Lenox Mall, this treasure, opened by chef Drew Van Leuvan, is one of Atlanta's most underrated restaurants (purely based on its location, I'm convinced)—even more surprising when you consider the chef's résumé reads like a who's who of culinary greatness (he apprenticed under chefs Jean-Louis Palladin, Guenter Seeger, and Wylie Dufresne; manned the stove at Atlanta's acclaimed Toast, Spice, and ONE. midtown kitchen). Named for the seven principles of architecture—sacrifice, truth, power, beauty, life, memory, and obedience, which Van Leuvan fancied were equally apropos in the kitchen—the communal, produce-driven menu might as well be an edible essay to made-from-scratch cooking (order the house-made charcuterie for proof). As expected, the pasta is outstanding (Van Leuvan started Pan De Mie Pasta, a handmade-pasta company that sold to 28 of the city's top restaurants)—go for the pesto-filled tortellini or (if it's in season) the agnolotti stuffed with sweet corn and mascarpone cheese, adorned with chanterelles and blueberries. Summer in a bowl. The mussels with smoky andouille, charred jalapeño, and fennel butter are a mainstay. So is the lobster bun, which is as tender and plush as the cocktail menu is electrifying. Sit on the patio—not that the warm, rustic interior isn't beautiful, but al fresco dining will reveal just what an oasis Seven Lamps truly is.

Twice-Cooked Cumin Chicken Wings with Charred Jalapeño Dressing

(SERVES 4)

8 cups water
1 cup salt
1 cup granulated sugar
3 tablespoons whole cumin seeds, divided
1 tablespoon red pepper flakes
4 sprigs thyme
20 chicken wings, wings clipped off and separated at elbow joints
8 jalapeño peppers
2 shallots, minced
2 cups mayonnaise (Duke's preferred)
1 cup water
2 tablespoons confectioners' sugar
2 tablespoons distilled vinegar
7 sprigs cilantro, chopped
4 Roma tomatoes, skins removed, finely diced
Salt and pepper to taste
2 quarts chicken stock
2 quarts vegetable oil for frying

In a large pot over high heat, combine 8 cups water, salt, granulated sugar, 1 tablespoon cumin seeds, red pepper flakes, and thyme. Bring to a boil, remove from heat, and allow to cool. Once cool, add the chicken wings and elbows to the brine and allow to soak in the refrigerator for 4 hours.

Meanwhile, heat a sauté pan over high heat. Once very hot, add the jalapeños and char the skin on all sides, about 3 to 5 minutes. Once charred, set aside and cool before dicing.

In a nonreactive bowl, combine the diced peppers with the next seven ingredients (shallots through tomatoes); mix well. Season with salt and pepper to taste. Reserve the jalapeño dressing.

Preheat oven to 300°F. Remove the chicken from the brine and place in a large ovenproof pot over medium heat. Cover with the chicken broth and bring to a boil. Place pot in the oven and cook for 1 hour. Remove from the oven and allow to cool. Toss the cooled chicken with the remaining 2 tablespoons cumin seeds.

Heat the oil in a heavy-bottomed pot or a deep fryer until a candy thermometer registers 375°F. Carefully place the chicken into the hot oil and fry until golden brown and crispy, about 4 to 5 minutes. Serve with the jalapeño dressing.

Salad of New Potatoes & Spring Peas

(SERVES 4)

8 new potatoes
Salt
1 cup sugar snap peas
1 cup snow peas
1 cup English peas
1 tablespoon extra-virgin olive oil
1 tablespoon unsalted butter
3 garlic cloves, thinly sliced
2 teaspoons red pepper flakes
8 pickling cucumbers, ends removed and halved lengthwise
2 sprigs fresh dill, chopped
1 tablespoon grated Asiago cheese

Place the potatoes in a medium pot and cover with water and a pinch of salt. Over medium heat, cook the potatoes until soft throughout, about 30 minutes. Remove the potatoes. Set aside. Discard the water.

In the same pot add 3 quarts of fresh water and bring to a boil over high heat. Add a pinch of salt and the sugar snap peas, snow peas, and English peas. Cook for 45 seconds and then place the peas in an ice bath to stop the cooking process. Reserve.

Preheat oven to 400°F. Heat an ovenproof sauté pan over medium-high heat with the olive oil and butter. Halve the potatoes and add to the pan. Place the pan in the oven for 3 minutes. Remove the pan from the oven and place back on the stove over medium-high heat. Add the blanched peas to the pan. Add the sliced garlic and red pepper flakes and toss until thoroughly mixed. Sauté until the peas are hot and the garlic is translucent, about 1 to 2 minutes.

Meanwhile, grill the cucumbers on a grill over high heat. Add the cucumbers to the potatoes and season with salt to taste. Serve, garnishing with fresh dill and Asiago cheese.

Southern Art & Bourbon Bar

3315 Peachtree Road NE
Atlanta, GA
(404) 946-9070
southernart.com

Owner and Executive Chef: Art Smith
Chef de Cuisine: Keoko Turner
Head Mixologist: Tokiwa "Toki" Sears

Atlanta has been home to some pretty famous restaurants over the years—Tom Colicchio, Emeril Lagasse, and Jean-Georges Vongerichten all set up shop in the Big Peach, but unfortunately none lasted. One celebrity chef seems to have found the winning formula. The former personal chef to Oprah Winfrey, Art Smith, who you may also recognize from *Top Chef* or one of his three award-winning cookbooks, opened his Southern-inspired restaurant, Southern Art, in the heart of Buckhead's business district (specifically, inside the InterContinental hotel) back in 2011. His secret? Maybe it's the deep-rooted family traditions Smith calls upon for his clean, simple menu (pecan-crusted trout and duck confit cassoulet are standouts). Perhaps it's the delicious regional country ham found at the restaurant's artisan ham-and-charcuterie bar, though it could easily be the vintage pie table dispensing delectable baked-to-order desserts. No doubt, the convivial Bourbon Bar offering more than 70 varieties and pre-Prohibition-era cocktails has something to do with it. Whatever his secret may be, we hope Southern Art is here to stay.

Buttermilk Biscuits

(SERVES 10)

5 cups self-rising flour
1 teaspoon baking powder
½ teaspoon sugar
½ cup shredded white cheddar
Pinch of chopped rosemary
Pinch of black pepper
Pinch of salt
4 tablespoons unsalted butter, diced small
½ cup buttermilk

Preheat the oven to 385°F. Mix all the dry ingredients with diced butter. Gently fold in the buttermilk until the dough begins to come together. Roll the dough about 1¼" on a flat surface and cut biscuits with a knife or cookie cutter. Bake for 12 minutes.

Buttermilk Fried Chicken

(SERVES 5)

½ cup kosher salt
1 gallon cold water, divided
1 teaspoon black peppercorns
3 sprigs rosemary
5 sprigs thyme
4 cloves garlic
2 bay leaves
2 whole chickens, cut into 10 pieces
1 quart buttermilk
6 large eggs
1 tablespoon hot sauce
2 teaspoons plus 1 tablespoon salt, divided
2 teaspoons ground black pepper
2 cups all-purpose flour
3 cups self-rising flour (White Lily preferred)
1 tablespoon garlic powder
1 tablespoon onion powder
2 tablespoons paprika
½ teaspoon cayenne
2 teaspoons dried thyme
Canola oil for frying

In a large soup kettle, dissolve ½ cup kosher salt in 2 cups water over medium-high heat. Add the remaining water, stirring to blend in the salt. Add the black peppercorns, rosemary, thyme, garlic, and bay leaves. Place the chicken in the brine and refrigerate for at least 12 hours. Transfer the chicken from the brine to a large bowl and submerge in the buttermilk. Refrigerate for 4 to 6 hours.

In a large mixing bowl, whisk together the eggs, hot sauce, 2 teaspoons salt, and pepper. Drain the chicken from the buttermilk and transfer to the egg wash, turning to coat.

In a separate bowl, mix together the flours, garlic and onion powders, 1 tablespoon salt, paprika, cayenne, and thyme. Add more salt, if needed, to taste.

Remove 2 pieces of chicken at a time from the egg wash, letting the excess liquid drain off. Roll the chicken in the seasoned flour, shaking off any excess flour. Lay the chicken on a wire rack until ready to fry, ensuring all excess flour is shaken off. Repeat with the remaining chicken pieces.

Pour 1 inch of canola oil into a large cast-iron pan and heat over medium heat until a candy thermometer registers 325°F. Carefully place 4 to 6 pieces of chicken into the hot oil, using long tongs to move the chicken and being careful not to crowd the pan. Cook until the chicken reaches an internal temperature of 180°F, turning each piece every 2 minutes. (*Note:* Be sure to give the oil 5 minutes to reach the proper temperature before dropping in the next batch of chicken.) Place the fried chicken on a plate lined with paper towels to absorb excess oil and keep at room temperature until ready to serve. Place the fried chicken on large serving platters and serve.

Pretzel Pie

(SERVES 8)

¾ cup sugar, divided
15 ounces heavy cream, divided
Pinch of sea salt
7 ounces finely crushed pretzels
5 ounces softened unsalted butter
1 egg yolk
5 ounces chocolate chips (65% bittersweet preferred)

At least a day before serving, in a sauce pot over medium heat, caramelize 4 ounces sugar by dissolving it in 1 tablespoon water. Cook until the mixture becomes a deep brown color, about 8 minutes, stirring often.

Meanwhile bring 7 ounces heavy cream to a boil in a medium saucepan. Deglaze the caramel with the boiling cream and add the sea salt. Remove the mixture from the stove and add 4 ounces cream, stirring to combine. Chill overnight in the refrigerator. The next day, whip the caramel cream like a chantilly (grainy texture).

Preheat oven to 350°F. In a small bowl, mix the crushed pretzels and butter together. Spread the mixture in a 10-inch pie mold. Bake for 8 minutes, remove from the oven, and let cool for 1 hour.

Meanwhile, in a sauté pan over medium-high heat, boil the remaining 4 ounces cream with the remaining 2 ounces sugar. Remove the pan from heat after the sugar is dissolved. Add the egg yolk and cook for 2 minutes. Add the chocolate to the top of the cream mixture, but do not mix yet. Wait 10 minutes, then mix the chocolate with the cream. Pour the mixture into the partially baked pretzel pie crust. Let set at room temperature for 4 hours. Garnish with the caramel cream.

Taqueria del Sol

taqueriadelsol.com
CEO: Mike Klank
Corporate Chef: Eddie Hernandez

1200-B Howell Mill Road
Atlanta, GA 30318
(404) 352-5811

359 West Ponce de Leon Avenue
Decatur, GA 30030
(404) 377-7668

2165 Cheshire Bridge Road
Atlanta, GA 30324
(404) 321-1118

There aren't many restaurants I'll wait in line for, but Taqueria del Sol is one of them. Granted the line moves quickly, and you can drink margaritas while you wait, but still. The sentiment remains: The food here, Southwest-inspired fare with a Southern flair, is worth the wait. Just try chef and Mexico-native Eddie Hernandez's Memphis taco, pulled smoky pork smothered in tequila BBQ sauce and topped with spicy jalapeño coleslaw, for proof. I'm also mad about the roasted chicken enchilada doused in pork green-chile sauce, though no meal is complete without the salsa trio (verde, asada, and fresca), buttery guacamole, and, of course, cheese dip. Did I mention each of these rings in under $5? Like I said: worth the wait. I'm certainly not alone in that conclusion—TDS has become so popular (they've sold nearly 1 billion tacos), they've added three more locations in Georgia (plus more in Pennsylvania and Tennessee) since opening the original in a former lawn-mower repair shop in the Westside Provisions District back in 2000.

Chicken Enchiladas with Lemon Cream Sauce

(SERVES 6; 2 ENCHILADAS PER PERSON)

For the chicken filling:

1 whole chicken, quartered
2 stalks celery, roughly chopped
1 small carrot, roughly chopped
2 tablespoons salt, plus more to taste
2 tablespoons margarine (or equal parts butter and vegetable oil)
1 medium onion, diced
2 cloves garlic, minced
1 bay leaf
2 cups chopped fresh tomatoes

For the lemon cream sauce:

3 cups reserved chicken stock (from above)
Juice of 1 large lemon (about 3 tablespoons)
½ cup roux (whisk ½ cup all-purpose flour into 1 stick melted unsalted butter)
1½ cups sour cream
Salt to taste

For plating:

½ cup vegetable oil
12 (6-inch) corn tortillas
2 cups shredded Monterey Jack cheese
Ground paprika
¼ cup sliced pickled jalapeños

To make the chicken filling: Place the chicken, celery, carrot, and 2 tablespoons salt in a large stockpot and cover with 2 quarts cold water. Bring to a boil over high heat. Reduce to a simmer and cook until the chicken is just done, about 25 minutes. (*Note:* Don't overcook, as the chicken will be cooked again.)

Remove the chicken from the pot and set aside to cool, reserving the stock. When the chicken is cool enough to handle, remove the skin and bones and return to the stockpot with the cooking water. Return to a boil and cook for an additional 20 minutes. Strain and reserve the stock. (*Note:* Stock can be prepared 1 day in advance; store the chicken and stock separately in the refrigerator.) Meanwhile, using two forks or your fingers, shred the chicken and set aside.

Heat the margarine in a large skillet over medium heat. Add the onion, garlic, and bay leaf and cook until onions are soft, about 5 minutes. Add the tomatoes and cook 2 minutes. Stir in 5 cups shredded chicken (reserve the rest for another use) and salt to taste.

To make the lemon cream sauce: In a 2-quart saucepan, bring the chicken stock from above and lemon juice to a boil. Stir in the roux, a spoonful at a time, until the stock is very thick (you may not need all of the roux). Remove the saucepan from the heat, stir in the sour cream, and season to taste with salt.

To assemble the enchiladas: Preheat the oven to 350°F. In a small skillet over medium-high heat, add enough vegetable oil to cover the bottom. Place 1 tortilla in the oil and cook until the tortilla begins to bubble, about 30 seconds. Use tongs to gently turn the tortilla. Heat another 30 seconds and place the tortilla on paper towels to drain. Repeat with the remaining tortillas, adding vegetable oil as necessary to the skillet and layering the tortillas on paper towels to drain.

Place about ½ cup of the chicken filling in the center of a tortilla. Roll it tightly and place it, seam side down, in a 9 x 13-inch baking dish. Repeat with the remaining tortillas and filling, arranging tightly in the dish so they all fit. Cover the tortillas with the sauce, and sprinkle the top evenly with the cheese. Bake until bubbly and beginning to brown, about 30 minutes.

To plate: Place an enchilada on a plate. Sprinkle with paprika and top with 3 slices of pickled jalapeño.

Oyster Tacos with Jalapeño Coleslaw

(SERVES 6)

For the sauce:

¼ onion
½ cup chopped celery
2 jalapeños, chopped
2 cups mayonnaise
1 tablespoon Tabasco Sauce
¼ finely diced red bell pepper (with seeds, but veins removed)
¼ finely diced yellow bell pepper (with seeds, but veins removed)
¼ finely diced green bell pepper (with seeds, but veins removed)
1½ cups sweet pickle relish
Salt and pepper to taste

For the jalapeño coleslaw:

9 cups chopped green cabbage
¾ cup grated carrots
1 tablespoon diced pickled jalapeño
½ tablespoon black pepper
1 cup mayonnaise
½ cup sugar
Juice of 1½ lemons
Salt to taste

For the oysters:

1 cup all-purpose flour
2 cups ground blue cornmeal
½ cup cornstarch
¼ tablespoon baking powder
1 tablespoon salt
12 Gulf oysters, shucked
2 quarts vegetable oil
6 (6-inch) flour tortillas

To make the sauce: In food processor, pulse the onion, celery, and jalapeños. Transfer the mixture to a medium bowl and add the mayonnaise, Tabasco, bell peppers, and pickle relish. Mix well and add salt and pepper to taste. Refrigerate for 3 hours.

To make the coleslaw: In a large mixing bowl, combine all the ingredients and mix well. Set aside.

To make the oysters: In a shallow dish, mix the flour, cornmeal, cornstarch, baking powder, and salt. Coat the oysters in the mixture.

Heat the oil in a deep fryer until a candy thermometer reads 375°F. Carefully add the coated oysters to the hot oil and fry until golden and cooked through, about 2 to 3 minutes. Drain the oysters on paper towels.

To plate: Top the tortillas with the fried oysters, sauce, and jalapeño coleslaw. Serve.

The General Muir

1540 Avenue Place, Suite B-230
Atlanta, GA 30329
(678) 927-9131
thegeneralmuir.com

Co-Owner and Executive Chef: Todd Ginsberg

Atlanta and *Jewish deli* aren't words you typically hear uttered in the same sentence. At least not before Todd Ginsberg, a Culinary Institute of America grad who trained under Michelin-starred chefs Lucas Carton and Alain Ducasse before cheffing at Atlanta's Bocado, opened The General Muir. Named for the transport ship that brought co-owner Jennifer Johnson's (of West Egg Café) refugee family to the United States in 1949, The General Muir is a modern marriage of classic New York Jewish delis (think house-cured pastrami, hand-rolled bagels, and smoked trout) and fun farm-to-table small plates, like gooey poutine with brisket-spiked gravy and swiss chard fritters. The gorgeous cafe is seemingly open all day (breakfast, lunch, dinner, and weekend brunch), complete with locally roasted Batdorf & Bronson coffee, a counter-service deli and bakery, and Friday-night-only fried chicken dinners (dubbed by the *AJC* "a Southern vision of Sabbath dinner"). Ginsberg, the James Beard nominee and man behind Bocado's original cult-inducing burger, also brought his patty-prowess with him—this version contains gruyère, caramelized onions, pastrami, Russian dressing, and pickles. Mazel tov, chef. You done good.

Swiss Chard Fritters

(SERVES 10)

10 pounds swiss chard
Salt to taste
2 cup all-purpose flour
1 tablespoon baking powder
Pepper to taste
1 egg
1 cup whole milk
1 cup shredded Parmesan cheese, plus additional for garnish
Canola oil for frying
1¼ cups ricotta

Separate the stems of the swiss chard from the leaves and reserve about one-third of the stems. In a large pot of boiling salted water, blanch the chard leaves until the color turns a bright green, about 90 seconds. (*Note:* Blanch the chard in batches as to not overcrowd the blanching pot.) Shock the blanched leaves in ice water, drain, and squeeze out as much as possible. Finely chop the leaves.

In a large bowl, combine the flour, baking powder, and salt and pepper. In another bowl, combine the chopped chard, egg, milk, and Parmesan. Add one-third of the dry mixture to the chard mixture, mixing together with a wooden spoon. Repeat until all of the dry mixture has been incorporated into the chard. Adjust seasoning once all of the flour has been incorporated. Allow the batter to rest for 30 minutes.

Meanwhile, cut the reserved chard stems into rectangles. Cook stems until tender, about 35 minutes. Drain, and transfer chard stems to a sheet pan, arranging them in an even layer, to cool. Once cooled, cover stems with Parmesan and place under a broiler set to 500°F until golden brown, about 2 minutes. Set aside.

Heat 4 inches of oil in a heavy-bottomed pot or a deep fryer until a candy thermometer registers 350°F. Carefully lower tablespoon-size balls of batter into the hot oil in batches so as not to overcrowd the fryer. Fry until golden brown, about 2 minutes. Drain the fritters on paper towels.

Divide ricotta evenly among 10 plates, about 2 tablespoons per plate. Place fritters on top of ricotta. Garnish with Parmesan cheese. Top with the broiled chard stems. Serve.

Pecan-Crusted French Toast with Roasted Bananas & Spiced Butter

(SERVES 2)

For the spiced butter:

½ pound (2 sticks) unsalted butter, slightly softened
Zest of half an orange, grated with a Microplane
½ teaspoon ground cinnamon
Pinch of salt

For the french toast:

1½ cups coarsely ground cornflakes (not too fine, not too pebbly)
1½ cups coarsely ground pecans (not too fine, not too pebbly)
4 eggs
⅛ cup heavy cream
⅛ teaspoon vanilla extract
4 (1-inch thick) slices challah (can substitute brioche)
2 ounces clarified butter (can substitute half butter and half canola oil)
1 large banana, peeled and quartered lengthwise
2 tablespoons dark brown sugar, packed
Maple syrup for drizzling

To make the spiced butter: Place the butter in the bowl of a stand mixer fitted with the paddle attachment. Mix at medium-high speed until smooth, about 3 minutes. Add the orange zest, cinnamon, and salt. Mix at high speed until thoroughly combined, about 2 to 3 minutes. Pack the butter into a ramekin. Cover and chill in the refrigerator until ready to serve. (*Note:* Leftover butter can be stored in the refrigerator for up to 1 week, or frozen indefinitely.)

To make the french toast: Preheat the oven to 350°F. Place the ground cornflakes and pecans in a pie plate or flat bowl and toss to combine. Set aside.

Crack the eggs into another pie plate or flat bowl. Add the cream and vanilla and whisk until frothy and well combined.

Dip each slice of bread in the egg mixture, making sure to coat evenly on both sides. (*Note:* To get a thorough soak, you may need to let the bread rest in the egg for a minute or two per side. You want the bread to be soaked but not overly soggy and gooey.) Place the bread into the cornflake-pecan mixture and press gently so that it's coated on all sides.

Heat clarified butter in a large ovenproof skillet over medium heat. Brown the bread on both sides, about 3 to 4 minutes per side. Place the skillet in the oven and bake until the bread puffs up and is just cooked through, about 5 to 8 minutes.

Place the bananas in a medium-size ovenproof pan or baking tray and sprinkle with brown sugar. Broil under high heat to melt the brown sugar and caramelize the bananas, about 5 minutes. If the sugar runs off, spoon it back on top of the bananas. (*Note:* You may also use a brûlée torch to caramelize bananas.)

Place 2 slices of the cooked toast on a plate. Top with caramelized banana slices and a generous pat or two of the spiced butter. Drizzle with maple syrup. Serve with more maple syrup on the side.

The Luminary

99 Krog Street, Suite Y
Atlanta, GA 30307
(404) 458-5636
TheLuminaryATL.com

Executive Chef and Owner: Eli Kirshtein
Partner and General Manager: Jeremy Iles

As I write this book, Atlanta-native Eli Kirshtein is hard at work getting his first restaurant ready to open. The Luminary, named after Atlanta's first newspaper, will be an American brasserie—it's also one of Atlanta's most anticipated restaurant openings according to *Eater*, *Zagat*, and *Atlanta* magazine. For good reason. Not only does Kirshtein's reputation precede him—the Culinary Institute of America grad has worked for superstar chefs like Kevin Rathbun, Jean-Georges Vongerichten, Eric Ripert, and Richard Blais in addition to starring on *Top Chef*—but The Luminary is expected to offer one of the city's more impressive beer lists (24 drafts and as many bottles, particularly American craft and Belgian) and raw bars (expect oysters, clams, crudos, and sky-high seafood towers). It's also located in Krog Street Market, one of Atlanta's hottest foodie destinations. "I wanted to open a restaurant with the food we want to eat," Kirshtein concedes. "Which is bistro fare, steak frites, chicken liver mousse, a raw bar, food with a sense of discipline. It's a unique concept with an old-school mind-set."

Steamed Georgia Shrimp with Leeks en Vinaigrette

(SERVES 4)

1 tablespoon whole-grain mustard
3 tablespoons sherry vinegar
½ cup grapeseed oil (can substitute canola oil)
1 tablespoon porcini oil
Salt and pepper to taste
1 pound Georgia white shrimp (21–25 size preferred)
1 teaspoon olive oil
salt to taste
2 large leeks, halved (root intact) and cleaned
2 tablespoons finely sliced chives

In a nonreactive bowl, combine the mustard and vinegar. Slowly whisk in both oils until emulsified. Season with salt and pepper to taste. Divide the vinaigrette and set aside in two separate bowls.

In a steamer, steam the shrimp (shell on) until just cooked, about 4 minutes. While still warm, remove the shells and place the meat in one of the vinaigrette bowls, tossing to coat. Allow the shrimp to cool slowly in the vinaigrette.

Preheat oven to 400°F. Lightly oil and salt the leeks on a baking sheet, cut side up. Bake until the leeks are just tender and slightly browned, about 15 minutes. Remove the leeks from the oven and slice into 1-inch lengths, discarding the root base.

Place the leeks evenly on four plates. Dress the leeks with the remaining vinaigrette and artfully place the shrimp on top, dividing it evenly among the plates. Garnish with the chives. Serve slightly warm, but not hot.

The Pinewood

254 West Ponce de Leon Avenue
Decatur, GA 30030
(404) 373-5507
pinewoodtr.com

Owner: Brooks Cloud
Partner & Executive Chef: Mike Blydenstein
Bar Director: Julian Goglia

When you're craving serious Southern comfort food, The Pinewood, an American whiskey-focused, pine-clad (every surface is literally made from pine, hence the name) neighborhood hangout in quirky Decatur, has you covered. Dishes are in constant rotation, but chef Mike Blydenstein, who has cooked with Southern icons like John Besh and Emeril Lagasse, puts his Creole lilt on kitschy staples like fried bologna sandwiches with house-made sour pickles, jumbo scallops swimming in andouille vinaigrette, and Disco Tots, taters tossed with tangy melted cheddar and fiery chicken gravy. The bar, helmed by pharmacist-turned-bartender Julian Goglia, is equally mouthwatering—look for over 100 kinds of whiskey, including unique, hard-to-find labels like Pappy Van Winkle, a mammoth bitters collection, and innovative house-made syrups, tinctures, infusions, and sodas. That's my kind of prescription.

Cornmeal-Crusted Catfish with Hoppin' John

(SERVES 4)

4 (6-ounce) catfish fillets, skin removed
Salt and pepper to taste
4 teaspoons yellow mustard
1 cup all-purpose flour
2 cups buttermilk
2 cups cornmeal seasoned with 1 tablespoon Creole seasoning (Zatarain's preferred)
Vegetable oil for frying, plus 2 tablespoons
½ cup finely diced applewood-smoked bacon
1 large yellow onion, finely diced
2 red bell peppers, finely diced
2 green bell peppers, finely diced
4 ribs celery, finely diced
2 cups fresh field peas, blanched in salted water (can substitute frozen if fresh aren't available)
1 teaspoon sliced garlic
1 jalapeño, finely diced
1 tablespoon Creole seasoning (Zatarain's preferred)
2 cups jasmine rice
1 quart chicken broth

Season the catfish fillets with salt and pepper. Using a pastry brush, "paint" the fillets with a thin layer of the yellow mustard, about 1 teaspoon per fillet. Dredge the catfish in the flour. Dip the catfish into the buttermilk until well-coated and then into the seasoned cornmeal.

In a heavy-bottomed frying pan over medium heat, add ¼ inch of vegetable oil. Panfry the fish until golden brown on both sides, about 3 to 4 minutes per side. Remove the fish from the pan and reserve on a paper towel–lined plate.

In a large saucepan fitted with a lid, render the bacon in 2 tablespoons vegetable oil over medium heat until just crispy, about 4 to 6 minutes. Add the next eight ingredients (onion through Creole seasoning). Sweat the vegetables until the onions turn translucent, about 6 to 10 minutes. Add the rice and stir to incorporate. Add the chicken broth and season to taste. Bring to boil, then cover and reduce heat to low and let steam for 20 minutes.

To serve, divide the Hoppin' John among four plates. Top with the fried fish.

Vanilla-Bourbon Bread Pudding

(SERVES 6–8)

3 cups whole milk, divided
4½ cups heavy cream, divided
¾ cup bourbon, divided
1½ teaspoons cinnamon
¼ teaspoon ground nutmeg
3 teaspoons vanilla extract, divided
8 eggs
¾ cup light brown sugar, packed
2 medium loaves challah bread or brioche, torn into 1-inch pieces
½ cup confectioners' sugar
1 tablespoon cornstarch

Preheat the oven to 325°F. In a large mixing bowl, combine 2 cups milk, 2 cups heavy cream, ½ cup bourbon, ½ teaspoon cinnamon, nutmeg, 2 teaspoons vanilla extract, 8 eggs, and light brown sugar. Whisk until smooth and the sugar is dissolved. Pour mixture over bread pieces in another large mixing bowl, combining with your hands to ensure the bread has absorbed all of the liquid.

Liberally spray a 12 x 10 x 3-inch baking pan with nonstick pan spray. Spread the bread mixture evenly in the pan and cover with foil. Bake until a pick or skewer pulls cleanly from the center, about 45 to 60 minutes.

While the bread bakes, make the bourbon sauce by dissolving the confectioners' sugar in 1 cup milk, 2¼ cups heavy cream, and 1 teaspoon vanilla extract in a medium saucepan over medium heat. Once mixture is simmering, add the remaining ¼ cup bourbon and cornstarch and slowly whisk to thicken the sauce.

To serve, drizzle the bourbon sauce over the baked bread.

Optional: Top with vanilla-bean ice cream or serve as a breakfast substitute for french toast and top with caramelized-spiced apples.

U Restaurants

urestaurants.net

Owner and Executive Chef: Riccardo Ullio

Escorpion

800 Peachtree Street NE
Atlanta, GA 30308
(678) 666-5198

Fritti

309 North Highland Avenue NE
Atlanta, GA 30307
(404) 880-9559

Sotto Sotto

313 North Highland Avenue NE
Atlanta, GA 30307
(404) 523-6678
sottosottorestaurant.com

The year was 1981. Atlanta was receiving an unexpected treasure: Italian immigrant Riccardo Ullio, who would go on to open one of Dogwood City's best, most authentic Italian restaurants. That restaurant would be Sotto Sotto, though it didn't open until years later. First, Ullio got his master's degree in environmental engineering from Georgia Tech—not exactly the background you'd expect after tasting his luxuriously creamy risotto. But Ullio had to put himself through school somehow, and he did so by working at California Pizza Kitchen (another surprising trajectory for a chef who's revered for his whole roasted fish). Ullio got a taste of something he liked in the restaurant industry and went on to work for Pano Karatassos at Pricci. Finally, it's 1999 and Sotto Sotto has opened its doors. Immediately the city fell in love with Ullio's traditional Italian flavors and age-old recipes, not to mention his award-winning wine list, a 200-bottle anthology. On the heels of his success, Ullio then opened Fritti, a Neopolitan pizzeria beloved as much for the Funghi di Bosco pizza (draped with San Marzano tomatoes, mozzarella, earthy mushrooms, and a drizzle of magical white truffle oil) as for the sausage *arancini*. Escorpion, a home-style Mexican tequila bar and cantina, followed. The fiery chicken *tinga* tacos and braised pork tamales are not to be missed! Be on the lookout for Ullio's latest venture—as this book goes to press, he's got a second pizzeria in the works.

Spaghetti Cacio e Pepe

(SERVES 4)

Salt
1 pound dried spaghetti
1 pound pancetta, thickly diced
1 tablespoon olive oil
2 cups grated Pecorino Romano
Cracked black pepper to taste

Fill a large pot with salted water and bring to a boil over high heat. Cook the spaghetti until al dente, about 2 minutes less than package instructions. Drain, reserving some of the pasta water.

Meanwhile, in a sauté pan over medium heat, sauté the pancetta in olive oil slowly until golden brown on the outside, about 5 minutes. Toss the pancetta and oil with the cooked spaghetti and a bit of pasta water. Add the cheese, reserving some for the table, and black pepper. Serve immediately.

Seared Scallops & Cannellini Beans

(SERVES 4)

1 cup dry cannellini beans
1 tablespoon diced carrots
1 tablespoon diced celery
1 tablespoon diced onions
1 tablespoon olive oil
Sachet of thyme, bay leaf, and black peppercorns
1 pound dry-packed U-10 jumbo sea scallops
¼ cup diced fresh tomato
½ cup arugula leaves
Dash of truffle oil

Soak the cannellini beans in cold water overnight. Rinse and drain the beans.

In a sauté pan set over medium-high heat, sauté the carrots, celery, and onions in olive oil until wilted, about 5 to 7 minutes. Add the beans and sachet and cover with water. Bring to a boil, then reduce heat to low and simmer until the beans are tender but not mushy, about 1 to 1½ hours. Season with salt two-thirds of the way into the cooking process. Remove the pan from heat and let the beans cool in their own liquid.

In a nonstick pan over very high heat, sear the scallops until they are brown on both sides, about 2 minutes per side.

To serve, reheat the beans with some of their liquid, adding the tomato, arugula, and a touch of truffle oil. Pour the beans over the seared scallops. Serve immediately.

Panna Cotta with Caramel Sauce

(SERVES 6)

10 grams gelatin sheets
½ cup ice water
4 cups heavy cream
7 ounces sugar
¼ teaspoon lemon zest
½ vanilla bean, split lengthwise
8 coffee beans
1 cup sugar
1 cup water

Begin softening the gelatin sheets by immersing them in ice water. In a saucepan over medium-high heat, combine heavy cream, sugar, lemon zest, vanilla bean, and coffee beans and bring to a boil. Add the gelatin and stir well. Strain the liquid into stainless steel forms (can substitute ceramic ramekins) and chill in the refrigerator until set, about 4 hours.

Meanwhile, in a copper or stainless steel saucepan over high heat, cook the sugar until it becomes a medium-brown caramel color, about 4 minutes. (*Note:* Do not let the sugar crystallize.) Pour the water slowly into the caramelized sugar while whisking constantly until a sauce consistency is achieved. (*Note:* Be very careful as the caramel will bubble and pop and can cause severe burns.)

Unmold the panna cotta onto a plate by placing the forms briefly in hot water. Drizzle with the caramel sauce. Serve.

Umi

3050 Peachtree Road NE
Atlanta, GA 30305
(404) 841-0040
umiatlanta.com

Partners: Charlie Hendon, Farshid Arshid, and Fuyuhiko Ito
Executive Chef: Fuyuhiko Ito
Chef de Cuisine/Pastry Chef: Lisa M. Ito

There are so many things you should know about Umi. First and foremost, it is indisputably Atlanta's superlative sushi restaurant. The freshness (shipments of jet-fresh fish from Japan's famous Tsukiji Market are flown in daily), mastery (Tokyo-born chef Fuyuhiko Ito's precise knife skills and rice finesse are inimitable), and variety (more than two dozen fish species behind the counter) are unrivaled in Atlanta. You can truly taste the difference, whether you opt for yellowtail sashimi crowned with jalapeño, miso-marinated black cod, or melt-in-your-mouth otoro tuna drizzled with truffle oil (though I'm partial to the omakase menu, where chef picks). You should also know the restaurant is stunningly beautiful, thanks to partner Farshid Arshid's impeccable taste—he worked with local artist Todd Murphy to create the 23-foot custom white-oak sushi bar (the best seat in the house) anchoring the dazzling dining room, which is enveloped in hand-charred cypress walls adorned with gorgeous photography and striking chandeliers. You should also know that Umi provides unexpected creature comforts rarely found in sushi restaurants, like an incredible dessert menu (chef Lisa's green tea soufflé never fails to impress), a first-class cocktail program (the ginger-heavy Moscow Mule is my personal

favorite), and even tableside coffee service from Lamill Coffee. But, most importantly, you should know the people who make Umi possible are the most kind, hospitable souls I know. By my second visit, chef Ito knew my name. By my third, he and Lisa were helping me plan my honeymoon to Tokyo. They care about their customers, and I know I'm not alone. I see chef Ito watching his guests eat, noting their likes and dislikes, sending out often overlooked fish to introduce them to something new, asking them questions about their life. No chef looks as happy behind his station as Ito does at his sushi counter. Umi is truly a labor of love—the restaurant even exists solely because Arshid and Charlie Hendon convinced Ito to team up with them after his former digs, MF Buckhead, closed. Cue the hallelujah chorus, and save me a seat.

Black Cod Misoyaki

(SERVES 2)

½ cup sugar
1 cup mirin
½ cup sake, boiled about 3 minutes to evaporate alcohol and chilled
1 cup white miso
1 tablespoon salt
10 ounces black cod, filleted and cut into 1-inch slices
1 lemon for garnish

In a nonreactive bowl, mix the sugar, mirin, and sake together until the sugar is dissolved. Chill in the refrigerator for 1 hour. Add the mixture to the white miso and puree in a food processor until smooth. Set aside.

Lightly salt the cod and allow to dehydrate at room temperature for 15 minutes. Rinse the fish in cool water to remove all of the salt and dry with a paper towel. Pour three-quarters of the white miso marinade over the fish and marinate in the refrigerator for 2 to 4 days.

Remove the fish from the marinade and place on a grill preheated to 425°F. Cook until well-done, about 5 to 6 minutes per side. Carefully place the fish on a plate with the remaining white miso dressing on the side. Garnish with a squeeze of lemon.

Avocado Salad with Wasabi Vinaigrette

(SERVES 2)

½ cup rice vinegar
6 tablespoons prepared wasabi paste
¼ cup sugar
2 tablespoons salt
4 tablespoons canola oil
1 perfectly ripe avocado, halved, pit removed
½ cup sliced onions
1 lemon for garnish

In a nonreactive bowl, combine the vinegar, wasabi, sugar, and salt, whisking to combine. Drizzle in the oil and whisk until emulsified. Set aside.

Score the avocado with a knife to allow the dressing to better absorb. Place each avocado half on a plate covered with the sliced onions to stabilize the avocado. Pour wasabi vinaigrette in the dimple of the avocados. Garnish with a squeeze of lemon.

Optional: To make the salad more of a complete meal, you can add fresh crabmeat or shrimp to the top.

Varuni Napoli

1540 Monroe Drive NE
Atlanta, GA 30324
(404) 709-2690
varuni.us

Co-Owner and Chef: Luca Varuni
Co-Owner and Architect: Arturo Giancarlo Pirrone

When I first met Luca Varuni, he was seated across from me watching as I devoured his classic Margherita pizza (simplicity at its best). A little girl bounded over, snuggling up close to the Naples native, who whispered sweetly into her ear. "Is that your daughter?" I asked between sips of Prosecco. "No, a customer's, but we're all family here," Varuni responded in an accent so charming, I swear, the table of girls next to us simultaneously began batting their eyelashes. I looked around me—indeed the gorgeous patio was filled with families, the children of which Varuni invites into the kitchen to cook with him. This was some place special. This was Varuni Napoli, Morningside's newest Neapolitan pizzeria, the brainchild of architect Arturo Giancarlo Pirrone and Varuni, an Antico-alum who trained at Pizzeria La Notizia, the only Michelin-rated pizzeria in the world. Inside, it's theater as much as food. The interactive warehouse space houses two imported, handmade wood-fired brick ovens manned by Varuni's friends from Naples who followed him to Atlanta. If the weather isn't cooperating, the 24-seat pizza bar is the best spot to get a glimpse of the action (and sometimes a sound bite of Varuni singing). In true Italian fashion, the wine list is incredibly affordable (glasses begin at just $4 and bottles at $22), and a small market offers imported San Marzano sauce, buffalo mozzarella, flour, and oil.

Peperoni Imbottiti

(Stuffed Peppers)

(SERVES 4)

1 small onion, peeled and chopped
8 tablespoons extra-virgin olive oil, plus more for drizzling
⅝ cup ground beef
⅝ cup ground pork
2 cups dry white wine, divided
2 tablespoons fresh Italian parsley
½ cup Pecorino Romano
⅝ cup smoked shredded mozzarella
1½ tablespoons salt
1½ tablespoons black pepper
4 red bell peppers, top, stem, and seeds removed (reserve tops)

In a saucepan over medium heat, sauté the onion in olive oil until translucent, about 1 minute. Add the ground beef and pork and cook slowly for 15 to 20 minutes. Add 1 cup white wine and continue cooking for 20 minutes. Transfer the meat from the pan to a large bowl and add the parsley, Pecorino Romano, mozzarella, salt, and pepper. Mix well and allow mixture to cool.

Preheat oven to 300°F. Arrange the peppers, cut side up, on a baking sheet. Divide the meat mixture evenly among the peppers and close with the tops. Drizzle the peppers with additional olive oil and the remaining 1 cup wine. Bake for 1 hour. Serve.

Parmigiana di Melanzane

(Eggplant Parmesan)

(SERVES 4)

10 ounces extra-virgin olive oil, divided
3 small cipolline onions, julienned
7 pounds bone-in pork and beef ribs
1 cup dry white wine
27 ounces San Marzano tomato sauce
14 ounces Italian tomato paste
3 tablespoons salt
Sprig of basil, plus 3 tablespoons, chopped
3½ pounds Italian eggplant, cut into ¼-inch slices
1½ pounds fior di latte, shredded (can substitute mozzarella)
16 ounces Parmigiano Reggiano, grated

Add 4 ounces olive oil to a large saucepan over medium heat. Add the onions and ribs and sauté for 20 minutes. Add the white wine and cook until evaporated, about 15 minutes. Add the tomato sauce, tomato paste, salt, and basil sprig, and cook over medium heat for 3 hours, stirring every 5 to 10 minutes to prevent the ragù from sticking.

In a 10-inch sauté pan over medium heat, add 6 ounces olive oil. Once hot, add the eggplant slices and lightly fry for about 40 seconds per side. Set aside.

Preheat the oven to 300°F. In a large roasting pan, spread 2 cups ragù into an even layer. Add an even layer of fried eggplant slices over the ragù. Top the eggplant slices with an even layer of the fior di latte, Parmigiano Reggiano, and 1½ tablespoons basil. Repeat for the second layer. Bake for 20 minutes. Serve.

Neapolitan Pizza Dough

(SERVES 4)

5 grams yeast
4½ cups water
50 grams fine sea salt
8 cups "00" flour

Dissolve the yeast in the water by rubbing it between your fingers. Once the yeast is completely dissolved, add the salt. Slowly add the flour to the water and begin mixing by hand in a circular motion for 25 minutes. (*Note:* You can also use a mixer on low speed for 20 minutes.)

Press the dough with your hands, forming a round crust. Push accumulated air to the edge without squeezing the edge, as it needs to have a thickness of ¾ inch or less. The middle of the crust should be less than ¼-inch thick.

Preheat the oven to 500°F. (*Note:* At the restaurant, chef Varuni cooks his pizza in 900°F ovens.) Add your favorite toppings to the pizza and bake for 6 minutes.

Festivals and Events

Any food town worth its salt plays host to a handful of finger-licking festivals, and Atlanta is no different. From the Atlanta Food & Wine Festival, a culinary extravaganza devoted to exploring Southern food traditions through tasting tents, demos, seminars, and special dinners, to the Field of Greens Festival, a family-friendly lollapalooza featuring Georgia's best farm-to-table restaurants, complete with an interactive kids' village, live music, and a pig roast, there's something for every palate. Cityfolk can head to Taste of Atlanta, a three-day epicurean blowout in Midtown, for live demos, hands-on cooking classes, and bites from the city's top chefs; suburbanites are sure to find a taste of something they like at Taste of Roswell, a free fiesta in historic Roswell Square. Food-truck fanatics will revel in the Atlanta Street Food Festival, the largest gathering of food trucks (there are more than 40) in the Southeast in the heart of Piedmont Park, while beer aficionados will love the Sweetwater 420 Fest, a dangerously delicious jamboree in Centennial Olympic Park, with a 5K race to boot!

The Atlanta Food Truck Park & Event Center

Atlanta is a driving city, through and through. So food trucks have had a tough go of it in the Big Peach—between the lack of foot traffic and some less-than-truck-friendly laws, ours is a city that felt left behind from the mobile movement taking hold in western cities like Portland and Austin. That was until 2012, when the Atlanta Food Truck Park & Event Center took over a grassy field at the corner of Howell Mill. Now this Westside wonder is home to the largest food-truck park on the East Coast and Atlanta's first and only permanent park dedicated to showcasing portable provisions year-round. Typically, half a dozen trucks show up during the week (though the park is closed on Monday), while 20-plus trucks convene every weekend. With the largest international offering of any park in the country, there's no better place to be when the sun is shining than on a picnic blanket filled with Indian street food from Masala Fresh, Caribbean jerk chicken from One Love Jamaican Grille, Southern 'cue from Sweet Auburn BBQ, and Latin arepas from WOW! Food Truck. There's also live music, bocce ball, and free on-site parking—now you have no excuse.

Watershed on Peachtree

1820 Peachtree Road NW
Atlanta, GA 30309
(404) 809-3561
watershedrestaurant.com

Owners: Ross Jones and Emily Saliers
Partner and Executive Chef: Joe Truex

Watershed is one of Atlanta's most storied restaurants. When it opened back in 1998 in a converted gas station in Decatur, the restaurant was a major pioneer in the farm-to-table movement, earning a James Beard award for its novel efforts. It was (and still is) co-owned by Grammy-winner Emily Saliers of the Indigo Girls, and, at the time, the acclaimed Scott Peacock, who cooked for two Georgia governors and learned the secret to true Southern food from Edna Lewis (a legendary African-American chef beloved for her traditional cookbooks), ran the kitchen. Peacock and Lewis's lionized friendship is another story that could fill this entire book. But today, Watershed looks much different. For starters, it's now located in the historic South Buckhead neighborhood of Brookwood Hills inside Atlanta's only LEED-certified high-rise condo. The menu tells a different story, too. Chef Joe Truex, a Culinary Institute of America grad who cooked at NYC's Le Cirque under chef Daniel Boulud before opening Repast (a French-meets-Japanese eatery) in Atlanta, puts his Louisiana inflection onto his plates, which extend well beyond the South (just look at the country-ham-wrapped shrimp a la plancha or the roasted duck breast with foie gras and cornmeal crepes). "Now, we're more reflective of the new South, which is more multicultural and inventive with what's growing here," says Truex. But some things never change—the fried chicken on Wednesday is still as popular as ever. No surprise considering the saltwater-and-buttermilk-brined birds earned a maniacal following back in Decatur. Don't miss the Sunday Creole Jazz Brunch, a delicious spectacle complete with a jazz trio and roast beef po' boys.

Shrimp & Crabby Burger

(SERVES 8)

For the remoulade sauce:

1 cup mayonnaise
2 tablespoons chopped capers
2 tablespoons chopped cornichons
1 tablespoon finely chopped shallots
1 tablespoon Dijon mustard
½ ounce red wine vinegar
1 tablespoon chopped parsley
Salt and pepper to taste

For the burgers:

½ cup chopped scallions
1 tablespoon minced garlic
1 tablespoon unsalted butter
¼ cup water
2 teaspoons Old Bay Seasoning
2 teaspoons Worcestershire sauce
1 teaspoon salt
2 pounds 26–30 shrimp, peeled, deveined, and tails removed, divided
1 pound lump crabmeat
Zest of 1 lemon
2 tablespoons olive oil
8 hamburger buns, toasted (Holeman & Finch preferred)
Bibb lettuce

To make the remoulade sauce: In a medium bowl, combine mayonnaise, capers, cornichons, shallots, Dijon mustard, red wine vinegar, and parsley. Mix well and season with salt and pepper to taste.

To make the burgers: In a sauté pan over medium heat, sauté the scallions and garlic in the butter until soft, about 3 to 4 minutes. Remove from pan and let cool.

In a small bowl, mix the water with the Old Bay, Worcestershire, and salt. Set aside.

In a food processor, place 1 pound shrimp and puree until smooth. With the motor still running, add the seasoned water mixture and puree until smooth. Transfer to a large mixing bowl. Dice the remaining shrimp and add to the mixing bowl along with the scallion mixture, crabmeat, and lemon zest. Mix well until incorporated evenly and shape into eight 6-ounce patties.

In a large sauté pan, add 2 to 3 inches of water. Bring to a simmer and add the patties. Poach for 5 minutes. Remove the patties and add to an ice water bath to cool. Remove and reserve.

In a large cast-iron skillet, sear the patties over medium-high heat in olive oil until cooked through, about 3 to 4 minutes per side.

Add the seared patties to the hamburger buns and garnish each with 1 tablespoon remoulade and Bibb lettuce.

Optional: Serve alongside coleslaw and french fries.

WEST EGG CAFÉ

1100 HOWELL MILL ROAD
ATLANTA, GA 30318
(404) 872-3973
WESTEGGCAFE.COM

OWNERS: BEN AND JENNIFER JOHNSON AND SHELLEY SWEET
EXECUTIVE CHEF: WAYNE RHEINLANDER

When it comes to breakfast in Atlanta, there are few places as universally loved as West Egg Café, though you'll find a lot more than standard scrambled eggs here. Situated in the heart of Atlanta's bustling Westside, the open-all-day cafe serves up Southern comfort on a plate—go for the fried green tomato–egg wrap with tangy horseradish-dill sauce or the spicy black bean cakes smothered in smoky chipotle salsa, perfect alongside roasted garlic grits. For a sweet finish, there's no better option than the irresistible Coca-Cola cupcakes, which explains the inevitable line that forms outside for weekend brunch. The separate coffee shop, which brews locally roasted Batdorf & Bronson coffee, is another draw, especially when coupled with free Wi-Fi. You might go for breakfast, but it's easy to stay through dinner.

Chilaquiles

(SERVES 8)

For the sauce:

2 pounds Roma tomatoes, cored
2 pounds round tomatoes, cored
8 garlic cloves
2 teaspoons ground cumin
8 jalapeños
1 yellow onion, diced
Kosher salt and black pepper to taste

For the chicken:

2 pounds boneless, skinless chicken breast
2 jalapeños, roughly chopped
½ yellow onion, roughly chopped
Salt and pepper to taste

For plating:

20 ounces canola oil
¼ red onion, diced
1 (7.5-ounce) bag tortilla chips (homemade preferred)
16 sunny-side-up eggs
Sour cream for garnish
Queso fresco for garnish
Avocado slices for garnish

To make the sauce: Preheat the oven to 375°F. Place the tomatoes, garlic, and cumin in large stockpot and cover with cold water.

Spread the jalapeños and onions on a sheet pan and roast until slightly caramelized, about 20 minutes. Add the roasted vegetables to the stockpot over high heat and bring to a boil. Simmer over medium heat for 1 hour. Puree the mixture with an immersion blender until smooth. Season with salt and pepper. Transfer to a sealed container and refrigerate for at least 18 hours.

To make the chicken: Place the chicken in a large pot with the jalapeños and onions and cover with water; season with salt and pepper to taste. Bring to a rolling boil and cook until chicken is done, about 30 to 40 minutes. Strain the chicken and cool. Shred the chicken and set aside.

To plate: In a medium sauté pan over medium heat, heat the oil. Add the red onions and caramelize, about 3 minutes. Add the shredded chicken and reserved sauce and cook until hot, about 5 minutes. Add the tortilla chips, stir, and cook until chips have soaked up the sauce, about 3 minutes. Check seasoning and adjust to taste.

Transfer mixture to individual shallow ceramic dishes (like au gratin dishes). Top each dish with 2 eggs and garnish with sour cream, queso fresco, and sliced avocado.

Sweet Corn & Brown Sugar Bacon Pancakes

(SERVES 8)

12 bacon strips
½ pound light brown sugar
2 pounds canned sweet corn, drained
1 cup whole milk
1 cup granulated sugar, divided
3 extra-large eggs
2⅓ cups all-purpose flour
1¾ tablespoons baking powder
1 teaspoon kosher salt
Butter for cooking
Honey butter for garnish
Maple syrup for garnish

Preheat the oven to 350°F. Line a baking pan with parchment paper and arrange bacon strips side by side. Evenly coat the strips with the brown sugar and bake until bacon is cooked and glazed with brown sugar, about 15 minutes. Allow to cool. Chop the bacon into small pieces and set aside.

In a large bowl, combine the corn, milk, and ½ cup granulated sugar. Puree with an immersion blender until smooth. Add the eggs and blend just enough to break the eggs up. Set aside.

In a large bowl, sift the flour. Add baking powder, the remaining ½ cup granulated sugar, and salt.

Stir the wet ingredients into the dry ingredients just until the flour disappears, being careful not to overmix.

Place a small amount of butter on a hot griddle. Once melted, pour ¼ cup of the batter onto the griddle and allow it to spread out. Sprinkle with chopped bacon. Turn the pancake once air bubbles appear. Serve with honey butter and maple syrup.

Woodfire Grill

1782 Cheshire Bridge Road
Atlanta, GA 30324
(404) 347-9055
woodfiregrill.com
Owner: Nicolas Quinones
Executive Chef: Tyler Williams
Sous Chef: Matt Weinstein

Woodfire Grill is a restaurant that's seen a lot of change, a lot of faces, a lot of menus. But it's remained a jewel in Atlanta's crown since 2002 throughout it all. When it first opened, chef Michael Tuohy brought his clean California style to the plate. When Tuohy returned to the West Coast, he sold the restaurant to Bernard Moussa and Nicolas Quinones, who soon partnered with chef Kevin Gillespie (now of Gunshow), but by 2013, Quinones was the sole owner, and Tyler Williams, who hails from Abattoir, the chef. I'm not surprised the warm, rustic restaurant revered for its wine list (with more than 400 wines spanning over a dozen countries) has had so much success, considering Quinones's approach. "The culture here is based on sustainability, which means supporting local agriculture,

humane animal husbandry and sustainable fisheries, and employing people who care deeply about dining," explains Quinones. "I pay everyone a fair wage, there are no low-skilled employees, and I only hire people who want to move forward: servers who want to become sommeliers, dishwashers who want to become chefs, chefs who want to open their own places. Advancing each individual is the key to sustainability."

Farm Egg Wellington

(SERVES 4)

1 teaspoon white vinegar
1 tablespoon kosher salt
4 farm eggs, room temperature
1 pound button mushrooms, rinsed, cleaned, and patted dry
3 tablespoons canola oil
1 tablespoon unsalted butter
2 shallots, minced
4 garlic cloves, minced
2 tablespoon chopped fresh thyme
1 fresh bay leaf
¼ cup dry sherry
Kosher salt and black pepper to taste
½ cup roasted mushroom stock (can substitute brown chicken stock)
1 tablespoon whole-grain mustard
1 teaspoon sherry vinegar
4 thin slices aged country ham
1 (8 x 12-inch) sheet puff pastry, cut into 4 equal pieces
1 egg yolk
2 tablespoons water
1 tablespoon Maldon sea salt

Bring 1 quart water to a boil in a medium saucepan over high heat. Add the vinegar and salt. Gently lower the eggs (in their shells) into the boiling water and cook for 6 minutes. Gently remove the eggs from the water and place into an ice bath (a medium bowl filled with 2 cups ice and 1 cup water). Allow the eggs to cool. Once cooled, very gently tap the eggs on the side of the bowl to create cracks all over the surface, being careful not to damage the egg. Return the cracked eggs to the ice bath and let sit for 1 hour.

Gently press your thumb against the base of the egg to crack, ensuring you get underneath the membrane between the shell and the white. Peel the shell and membrane away from the egg, being very gentle so as not to burst the yolk, which is in a soft gel state. Repeat with all of the eggs. Set aside.

In a food processor, pulse the mushrooms until finely chopped, but not pureed. Set aside.

Heat a wide-bottom pan over medium-high heat. Add the canola oil and heat for 1 minute. Add the finely chopped mushrooms in an even layer and leave undisturbed for 3 minutes. Stir well and allow to sit undisturbed for another 3 minutes. Reduce the heat to medium and cook until dry, about 5 minutes. Add the butter and allow to foam. Add the shallots, stir well, and cook for 2 minutes. Add the garlic, thyme, and bay leaf and cook for 1 minute. Increase the heat to high. Add the sherry wine and flame off the alcohol, scraping up any browned bits with a wooden spoon. Allow the sherry to reduce until dry, about 3 minutes. Season with salt and pepper to taste. Repeat this process with the stock. Adjust seasoning to taste. Add the mustard and sherry vinegar, stirring to combine. Remove from heat and allow to cool. Reserve.

Lay four 12 x 12-inch sheets of plastic wrap on a work surface. Center a slice of country ham 1 inch inside the bottom edge of the plastic square closest to you. Take 1 tablespoon of the mushroom mixture and press to form a thin layer covering the ham. At the bottom edge of the ham closest to you, place an egg on its side. Using the plastic wrap, gently roll the egg up and away from you. Continue rolling to encapsulate the egg in the ham until you're left with a tube of plastic. Pinch the plastic on both sides and push any air outward. Grasp the plastic between your thumb and the forefinger with each hand and roll the plastic away from you to tighten around the Wellington. (*Note:* Do not tighten too much or the egg will break.) Repeat the process three more times with the remaining ham, mushroom mixture, and eggs. Remove the Wellington from the plastic.

Lay 4 more 12 x 12-inch sheets of plastic wrap on a work surface. Place the 4 rectangles of puff pastry down on the plastic in the same fashion as the ham. Roll the puff pastry away from you to encapsulate the egg. Trim off any excess puff pastry, and pinch the sides to seal, trimming off the excess. Roll the plastic around the puff pastry as you did before, and place in the refrigerator for 20 minutes.

Preheat the oven to 500°F. Unwrap the Wellingtons and place them on a clean work surface. Beat the egg yolk and water together until well mixed. With a pastry brush, generously brush the egg wash onto the Wellington and sprinkle with Maldon salt. Transfer the Wellington to a greased cookie sheet, leaving plenty of room between each Wellington. Bake for 3 minutes. Rotate the pan 180° and bake until golden brown, about 3 minutes. Serve immediately.

Spring Pea Soup with Cardamom Marshmallow

(SERVES 4–6)

Kosher salt
½ cup local spring English peas
¼ cup sweet petite frozen peas
3 tablespoons picked mint leaves
Sugar to taste
5 tablespoons unsalted butter, divided
2 Vidalia onions, julienned
1 bay leaf
2 tablespoons lemon juice, plus more to taste
1 cup half-and-half
2 cups vegetable stock, chilled
500 grams coconut milk
5 grams agar (can find at local health food store)
2 large carrots, peeled
1 cup carrot juice
1 teaspoon minced ginger
1 tablespoon apple cider vinegar
4 baby carrots, shaved thin
¼ cup English peas, blanched
12 small mint leaves, picked from stems
12 freeze-dried peas (can find at local health food store)
12 nasturtium flowers (can substitute your favorite edible flower)
12 green pea tendrils
12 golden pea shoots
1 tablespoon lemon juice
2 tablespoons extra-virgin olive oil
Pepper to taste

Fill a medium stockpot two-thirds full with water and bring to a rolling boil over high heat. Season the water with salt very liberally. Add the English peas and cook for 1 minute. Transfer peas to an ice bath. Repeat with the sweet frozen peas. Blanch the mint for 10 seconds and transfer to the ice bath. In a blender, puree the peas and mint with a few ice cubes until smooth. Season with salt and sugar to taste. Pass mixture through a fine mesh sieve. Reserve.

Heat a saucepan over medium low and add 3 tablespoons butter, onions, bay leaf, and lemon juice. Season with salt. Cook slowly, stirring often, until the onions are translucent and soft, about 5 minutes. Add the half-and-half and cook until reduced by half, about 8 to 10 minutes. Remove the bay leaf and puree in a blender until smooth. Add the pea puree and vegetable stock and continue to puree until smooth. Adjust your seasoning with salt, lemon, and sugar if necessary. Reserve and cool.

Bring the coconut milk and agar to a rolling boil in a medium saucepot over high heat. Pour the mixture into a shallow bowl and refrigerate for 1 hour until it's formed into a brittle gel. Break these pieces up and place them into a blender. Puree until smooth and pudding like. Season with salt to taste. Place in medium squirt bottle. Reserve.

In a medium saucepan, combine the carrots, carrot juice, ginger, remaining 2 tablespoons butter, and apple cider vinegar. Boil over high heat until almost dry, about 6 minutes. Puree the mixture in a blender until smooth, adding a little water or apple cider vinegar if needed. Season with salt to taste. Place in a medium squirt bottle. Reserve.

In a large mixing bowl, combine the remaining ingredients (baby carrots through olive oil). Season with kosher salt and pepper to taste, and toss to combine. Divide the salad between four to six deep soup bowls, leaving an open area to pour the soup. Squeeze the coconut and carrot purees around the bowl.

Optional: Garnish with Cardamom Marshmallow (recipe follows). Pour the pea soup over the garnishes at the table.

Cardamom Marshmallow

200 grams sugar
50 grams water
25 grams liquid glucose
12 green cardamom pods, toasted
4 sheets gelatin
1 egg white
Pinch of kosher salt
1 tablespoon cornstarch
1 tablespoon confectioners' sugar

In a medium saucepan over medium heat, combine the sugar, water, glucose, and cardamom pods. Heat until the sugar is dissolved. Remove from heat and let steep for 1 hour. Gently heat the mixture again and strain out the cardamom. Keep warm; reserve.

Meanwhile, soak the gelatin sheets in ice water until soft, about 5 minutes. Squeeze the gelatin sheets to remove moisture and melt them in a small saucepan over low heat until liquid but not hot, about 10 to 12 seconds.

In a stand mixer with a whisk attachment, combine the egg white and one-fourth of the liquid gelatin. Whip at medium-high speed until soft peaks form. Slowly add half of the warm cardamom mixture, followed by half of the remaining gelatin mixture and a pinch of salt. Repeat this process until all the syrup and gelatin has been used. Continue whipping until you have voluminous stiff peaks.

In a small mixing bowl, combine the cornstarch and confectioners' sugar, mixing well. Dust a cookie sheet with half of this mixture and spread the marshmallow evenly over the dusted cookie sheet. Tap the cookie sheet on the work surface to remove any air pockets and dust with the remaining cornstarch-sugar mixture. Let sit at room temperature until set, about 2 hours. Cut into fun shapes and serve with the soup.

Index